Just Say No To Democracy

The Case for Soft Authoritarian Rule in the Early Stages of National Development

David Lightle

DEDICATION

This book is published posthumously in dedication to Dave Lightle, the Author.

With love,
- Taiwan Dollis, Le Moo, Boober, and Dave Jr.

CONTENTS

FOREWARD

I hear you.   That is one of the more counter-intuitive book titles you have ever laid eyes on. But trust me, it is not simply a gimmick to sell books. The knee-jerk premise of democracy held by Westerners does not jive with the reality of the history of democratic development within the context of nation-building. That is the premise of this book, and I will endeavor to make that case plainly for everyone to see.

As I finally put fingers to keyboard on this long-contemplated book project, Egypt is once again on fire and in the global news. President Mohammed Morsi, democratically elected for less than a year, was removed from power by the nation's powerful military and replaced with an interim council until new elections can be held. The military took action in the national interest after social unrest reached an intolerable point.

The typical Western knee-jerk reaction is to condemn the "coup" and demand either restoration of the elected guy, or at least to hold new elections, like yesterday. In Egypt's case, neither approach is workable for the long-term benefits of the nation.

For its part, the U.S. is already talking about invoking a law that prohibits economic aid to any country in which a democratically elected leader is overthrown by a military coup. And, on the news programs, one talking head after another, politicians and commentators from all sides of the ideological spectrum, are arguing that democracy needs to be restored in Egypt, pronto. That is insanity. For starters, the military coup law was undoubtedly written by well-meaning politicians but who have no clue how the world really works, and how democracy should be implemented in a developing country. Egypt is the epitome of all that is wrong with the view that "democracy must come first." The Arab Spring as a whole, for that matter, must be organic in nature, free from the democracy drug pushers in the West, lest the Spring become nothing more than a nightmarishly long, endless Winter.

In October 2013, The Obama Administration proved itself unable to depart from the positions of nearly every U.S. president before when he and his Secretary of State John Kerry confirmed that they would withhold economic support from Egypt until it holds new elections for its presidency. This bankrupt maneuver harks back to 1989, when a Republican U.S. president, George Herbert Walker Bush, treated the Russians the same way. Boris Yeltsin had led the quick revolution that brought down the Soviet state, and he naturally sought Western, mainly U.S., support for his fledgling government. But the answer was no, not until he had a democratically elected parliament installed. That was unfortunate on many fronts. But the result is clear: Russia entered an enduring period of political chaos as competing self-interests rose out of the former woodwork of Soviet suppression, stalling much of any hope for socio-economic progress. To this day Russia remains mired in discord, but with a dictator wannabe trying to worm his way back into Soviet style rule. It's like no lesson whatsoever was learned from Russia as the U.S. now heads down the same beaten path with Egypt.

It doesn't have to be this way. Indeed, there are some very workable models for development out there, but which go largely ignored by Westerners because we are too busy trying to impose our own values or systems, or even our delusions of our own systems, on others. By insisting that Egypt first be democratic from top to bottom, Westerners in general are totally ignoring not only the recent development success stories in East Asia, but also their OWN histories and records of development.

It is a shame because by approaching democracy ass-backwards, the developed nations are doing nobody a favor, least of all the developing guys. Such an approach keeps nations mired in an endless circle of instability and violence, factors which always hinder economic development, which should be the primary concern of ANY national leader in ANY developing country. If not, then they are hopeless, and will continue to wallow in abject poverty and violence with no end in sight.

The title of this book means what it says. Developing nations need to Just Say No to Democracy in the early stages of development. Human history has proven that nearly ALL developed nations put economics first while paying lip service to democratic institutions. Even we Americans lie to ourselves about our democracy. We profess to be God's gift to democracy, but in fact, our early national development did not fill that bill at all. As this work will show, we were authoritarian for at least the first 150 years of our existence, and only set out on a path toward full democracy when the authoritarian leaders decided it was time to share power with others. Sound kooky? Sorry, but it's one of those, uh, "inconvenient facts" that Ronald Reagan might have complained about.

This work will show what's wrong with conventional Western dominated views on democracy, and go on to demonstrate that there are better models to emulate than those being shoved down the throats of most developing nations today. We will also examine why many nations fail and others succeed, laying out the factors for both results plainly for all to see.

Clearly, the title of this work borrows from former First Lady Nancy Reagan's "Just Say No to Drugs" campaign. And for good reason. Democracy, as our book cover graphic shows, is like a drug. Westerners have certainly been addicted to it and deluded by it. It can clearly be shown that in the early stages of national development democracy is usually a very counterproductive thing, yet Westerners treat it as some sort of panacea drug to be shoved down the throats of developing nations. Maybe it's just something Westerners do to help themselves feel good about themselves. To hell with those being forced to take the drug.

While the subject of this book is clearly counter-intuitive, you will find the arguments within quite convincing. They are based on my more than thirty years working within the governments and corporate worlds of developing nations. My longtime experience in Taiwan is key to how I have formulated and argue the belief that developing nations MUST say no to democracy, and firstly get on with the business of raising their people out from under the throes of poverty and put on a course toward prosperity. The really neat thing about these models is that democracy naturally occurs on the heels of economic development. The models for such developmental outcomes exist, and we must no longer ignore them.

The relevance of this subject is unmistakable in today's volatile world. Nation-building efforts in Iraq, Afghanistan, Egypt and even Russia are burdened by the negative Western influence of the Democracy drug. In Iraq, for instance, can democracy really take root in a few years in a country that was frankensteined together artificially some 70 years ago and whose tribes have engaged in incessant warfare for millennia? Not! But there is the U.S., trying its best to defy the tried and true principles of nation-building, insisting on democracy first, wholly ignoring what has worked and what hasn't.

The stakes could not be any higher. Of the world's 195 or so nations, three-fourths are underdeveloped, with most of those mired in abject poverty and on the road to Nowhereville in terms of development. It's time for a wake up call.

In the course of this work, I will focus on key ingredients for success in nation-building, while also examining the reasons why most have failed and remain poor. Such factors as the Social Compact, and a new term coined by me—The Stakeholder Society—will be highlighted as the critical keys for stable national development. Because these two topics are critical to the dialog below, let's go ahead and define them now. A Social Compact is an agreement between say, a government and the people, that spells out the trade-offs that will set the tone for national development. In other words, for example, the Government will ask for concessions from the folks, which are in turn offset by the Government making promises to deliver, in this case, economic prosperity to the folks. Usually, the Government will ask for special security measures or controls or restrictions on civil and political liberties so long as it delivers on the promise of prosperity. The goal is stability so that the nation's economy can take root in the most conducive environment possible. The Stakeholder Society, meanwhile, is a phrase I coin here for the purpose of identifying that moment in national development when the authoritarian rulers realize they can make the transition to full democracy. In economic development, economists have what they call the "Turning Point," usually defined as around USD$12,000 in per capita GDP, which is the point a nation starts to function more like a developed (or in the old, now politically incorrect vernacular First World) country. My term is more comprehensive, and refers to the point at which the excluded classes now have socio-political and economic interests completely aligned with the ruling class, and thus they become stakeholders in the most important factor of national development—stability. In the coming pages I will argue that no nation can become prosperous without first reaching the Stakeholder Society milestone, and that full-blown democracy should not be attempted until after that milestone is reached. It's like buttoning up your shirt. If you get the first button wrong, the sequence is messed up and things go awry. Only with national development, the stakes are infinitely higher, than just looking like a slob.

So, the basic schematic is revealed: Have a workable Social Compact in place, pursue a Stakeholder Society in socio-economic terms, and worry about full democracy later. In fact, you don't have to worry about it; it comes naturally on the heels of economic prosperity, as the record in East Asia clearly shows. Here, we will use Taiwan as the best example of how this works.

Of course, not every country is alike, so no one is arguing that a set of unforgiving principles are absolutely what's needed. That does not mean, however, that it is okay to continue making huge fundamental mistakes, such as putting democracy first. We will focus much on the Taiwan model, and on what's happening in China today as it struggles to adopt a path very similar to the one taken by their former Nationalist foes in Taiwan. Indeed, dissecting the Chinese political model, be it the original form propagated by Dr. Sun Yat-sen during the 1911 republican revolution in China (and adopted by Taiwan), or the current course of China, which itself is emulating Dr. Sun's path, is extremely relevant to the argument that democracy necessarily should come later in development. In fact, it comes naturally if the right Social Compact is implemented well and the goal of the Stakeholder Society is reached first.

We will dwell much on the subject of Dr. Sun and his

Three Principles of the People, his blueprint for modernizing China. Unwittingly, Sun may have devised a set of basic principles that can apply to most nation-states, not just the Chinese condition. And, he may have been the perfect guy to arrive at such conclusions. A Western trained medical doctor, Sun was wedded to the concept of combining the best of Eastern and Western traditions in his formula for China. He had spent much of his early career in Hawaii, perhaps the best setting for the mixture of East and West, and also in Hong Kong, where British traditions melded nicely over time with Cantonese Chinese ones. Unlike Japan, which Sun had thought had gone too far to the Western side in its haste to modernize during the Meiji Period, Sun felt that China could retain much of its culture while letting that very culture gradually adopt and assimilate certain Western traditions of governance and economics. The result, The Three Principles, is an extraordinary work that has unfortunately gone largely unnoticed in the West. Its manifestation arose first on Taiwan, and now much of what Dr. Sun envisioned for the whole of China is unfolding on the China Mainland as well.

In addition, readers need to understand fully the difference between freedom and democracy. One U.S. president after another has confused the two, or at least thought that they should occur simultaneously in the nation-building process. Not so at all. Freedom is a foundational component, and can and does exist in nations that are not democratic. Perhaps one of the freest places on earth is the least democratic, and is talked about extensively in this work as one of the best examples to support the main assertions made here. I am talking about Hong Kong, of course. Basic freedoms, which we will argue do not include such things as climbing a fence at a nuclear power plant to protest nuclear power, are the foundations for any road map for successful nation-building. We can simplify it by saying freedom is being able to wake up each day and decide for yourself what you want to be, want to do, and so on. Beyond that, you start to enter the realm of civil rights. We will dwell on this subject often as we examine both successful and failed models of development.

And, speaking of failed models, such a conversation on development can never overlook what happened in the 20th Century. Marxism and Communism rose up to command nearly one-third of the world's inhabitants at one time, giving rise to a tremendously costly Cold War between Capitalism and Communism. Over time, however, the ugly truth about Communism's political nature became evident, as did the ideology's abject failure as an economic system. Along the same timeline, world economic power began to shift to East Asia, where Japan and the Four Tigers, and now China, had forged unprecedented economic prosperity, which then led to a blossoming of democracy (China still to come!). Communism was defeated for several reasons, but chief among them is the spectacular success of the East Asians, even in today's China, which has no signs of Communism anywhere to be seen, even though it is still ruled by a Communist Party. Many elements of the conflict between Capitalism and Communism provide fodder for the arguments made in this work, and my background in Communism gave me a leg up in understanding some of the key dynamics of the rise of say, Taiwan and Korea, in particular, and now China.

It is also worth mentioning upfront that another key aspect of national development is recognizing the difference in Eastern and Western views on human rights. In the West, people generally think human rights include the right to vote, the right to protest, and a host of other Amnesty International-backed civil and political rights. Not so in the East. The Chinese dominated traditional view of human rights lists far more basic things, such as the right to a roof over your head, food in your belly and public safety for the common good. Indeed, in the East, the "common good" takes on far more importance than it does in the West. These concepts and how they affect national development planning in the East are crucial to your understanding of the role democracy plays, and how and when it is played out, in the national development traditions of East Asia in particular.

One also needs to understand the difference between "totalitarian" and "authoritarian." For the former, think the Soviet Communist Party or the Communist Party in North Korea. Think Stalin, Mao, Ho and the Kim dynasty. Totalitarian generally refers to rule that seeks to control nearly all aspects of life in a society. There is usually zero political freedom in such a society, and very little personal freedom as well. In authoritarian states, there is much control versus total control, and it is possible for freedoms to exist outside the political realm. There are cases in history (and today) of hard authoritarianism (Pinochet in Chile) and soft authoritarianism, the kind which existed earlier in the Taiwan, Korea and Singapore models of development.

But totalitarian and authoritarian can also be like night and day in their difference. Think the Koreas. Look at satellite photos from before 1990, with the totalitarian North juxtaposed against the then authoritarian South. Night and day. The North is pitch black, as it remains today at night, and the South is lit up like Times Square! Successful authoritarian regimes provide a vast contrast to their totalitarian counterparts. I rest that case…

Perhaps one of the most shocking things you will read about in these pages is my "un-American" conclusion that one-Party rule may be essential in the early stages of national development. The East Asian models, the most successful ones known to date, certainly bear this out. My own observations in Taiwan and now China certainly do as well. Undoubtedly it is counterintuitive for any Westerner to think that way, but as you will see below, there is a strong case for one-Party rule, or strongman rule under certain conditions, in the early stages of economic development.

Finally, let's not forget where we are in terms of a historical timeline of how we humans have ruled ourselves over the millennia. The issue is "sovereignty," or who is the sovereign over the society or country. It is clear that the Age of Democracy is relatively new and in many ways still untested. In ancient times, perhaps as late as or up until say, the year 900 A.D. or so, man was largely ruled by theocracies in which a human often posed as a god to rule over man. In China's long dynastic tradition spanning more than two millennia, the emperor received his mandate to rule from Heaven. Caesar declared himself a god in

Rome. And the Mayans, Aztecs, Mesopotamians, Egyptians and most other ancient cultures featured god-like leaders. Over time, as science began to carve into the legitimacy of god-rulers, theocracy gave way to the more mundane autocracy, in which kings and queens generally ruled. That system lasted well into the 20th Century, but the age of democracy, heralded in by the French and American revolutions, began to change the tide against monarchies. The French Revolution definitely ended with a very rough false start for democracy. It was followed by some eighty years of strife, culminating in a return to emperor rule with Napoleon. The American Revolution spawned a more stable system, but one that could hardly be considered fully democratic as women and people of color were not participants. Throughout the 20th Century, democracy was tested over and over, especially in places like Latin American, where stability was the exception rather than the norm. Problems still persist today in nearly all democracies, mature ones included (many think the U.S. is horribly dysfunctional today, e.g.). The point here is to start with the notion that democracy is a relatively new phenomenon on the human scene, and remains very much untested in terms of its ability to remain as a viable form of government. Some like to say it's not perfect, but it's the best system out there. Maybe, maybe not.

For purposes of style, I prefer a conversational approach. Nothing overly cerebral, and certainly not academic. Just a light and breezy dialog, peppered with anecdotes from my experiences working with developing nations.

And before we move on, perhaps a few words about my credentials in writing this book. A 1980 graduate of Dartmouth College, I was the first American undergrad to study in both the Soviet Union and Communist China. I sandwiched a year in Taiwan in 1979 with studies in the Soviet Union in 1978 and was among the first group of American undergrads to go to Peking University in Spring of 1980. My college major was uniquely customized. Its formal title was "Sino-Soviet Area Studies," but my advisors and I nicknamed it "International Communism." Prior to graduation, and with fluency in Russian and Chinese under my tongue, I dare say I was the darling of the intelligence agencies. I was particularly singled out as a "perfect" candidate for the soon retiring Blackbird (SR-71)spy plane program, partly due to my physical condition (I was a miler and had a resting pulse at the time of 32!). But, as fate would have it, my marriage to my Taiwan sweetheart would put an end to those ambitions. After breaking relations with Taiwan on January 1, 1979, President Carter issued orders that pretty much precluded anyone with such ties to Taiwan from entering positions with the highest security clearances.

I decided to fight the Cold War with my pen instead of piloting an SR-71 spy plane. We moved back to Taiwan with a 16-day old baby girl, and I immediately found my calling with Taiwan's Government Information Office (a combination of our White House spokesman office and U.S. Information Agency). A unique opportunity presented itself, and I accepted the position as special assistant to Taiwan's then Government Spokesperson, James Soong, a young, trusted confidante of President Chiang Ching-kuo.

I chose that course over grad school, and I am ever glad I did. What could I have possibly learned about China and the Chinese in school that I would not learn ten times over working inside a Chinese government? Bai tuo! (That's Chinese for "Come on!") It was a great ride. I soon made myself indispensable to their efforts to communicate with the outside world, and settled in for the long haul. As a matter of disclosure here, I ended up spending a total of 19 years in Taiwan's service, two of them in Washington working as a lobbyist/promoter for Taiwan at The Hannaford Company, owned by Peter Hannaford, who had been the long-time communication adviser to Ronald Reagan. Peter became the main mentor in my professional life, along with James Soong and his deputy, Raymond Tai, back in Taipei.

In Taipei, I was put to work writing position papers, white papers, political ads, and being the ghost writer (in English) for President Chiang, Premier Sun Yun-suan, Soong and a host of ministers in the Cabinet. In short, my job was to have an encyclopedic knowledge of Taiwan (and the enemy—Mainland China). This is the period of time in which I became a fan of Taiwan's development model. But I certainly did not start out that way. When I first arrived in Taiwan I had just come from the Soviet Union. I was bewildered to find that Taiwan had many of the same political or civil restrictions that the Soviets employed. Taiwan's excuse was the island's precarious security situation vis-à-vis Communist China. But at first, I didn't like it, and often had arguments with my future father-in-law (among many others) about how bad Taiwan was for paying lip service to democracy but not practicing it itself.

But, by the time of my departure from Taipei at the end of May 1979, I had been converted. In hindsight, the reason is simple: While Taiwan did have extraordinary security measures that would make you question the extent of their political freedoms, one overriding fact was clearly evident: Taiwan was hugely prosperous, and with a mostly happy and satisfied populace, to boot. Once you learned what was really going on in Taiwan, you could understand the lack of democracy and the special controls that were in place. I became a huge fan of President Chiang, and will argue throughout these pages that he is one of history's top national development geniuses.

In 1986, I returned to Taiwan to work directly for the GIO again. I did that for two years, and then started to spread my wings outside of political communications by taking on work in marketing communications and branding. All the while, I kept my consultancy channels with various government offices, including GIO and even some of the KMT Party offices, where James Soong and Raymond Tai eventually landed.

Those on the business side, and perhaps some on the editorial side of world media circles know me best as the "architect" of the Made in Taiwan image. In 1990, the Government and private sector teamed up to do something about the nagging problem of the Made in Taiwan image as the butt of international jokes, mainly having to do with quality. It wasn't really about overcoming the jokes; rather, it was all about overcoming the huge economic burden that the bad image had placed on Taiwan's economy. I was the General Consultant on the project, which is now in its 23rd year, making it one of the world's longest running national image projects.

After I made a name for myself working on Taiwan's global image, I gradually started helping other countries with image problems or nation branding projects. I assisted New Zealand in 1990-91, eventually laying the foundation for their long running PURE campaign, and helped steer Thailand through the financial crisis of 1997, which was also the year I finally left the Made in Taiwan project.

In the 2000s, I switched my attention to Latin America, where sophomore Spanish in Tippecanoe High School came into play for me. I worked with Colombia between 2004-07, and with Panama in 2010.

Today, my professional life is divided between country image work and consulting for Chinese corporations that are seeking to become multinationals, handling mostly image issues, including branding, positioning and promotion. Along the way, I have more than 25 years experience working closely with the governments and private sectors of developing nations. The lessons learned form the basis of this book. I have had the incredible privilege of being tutored in national development by some of the all-time greats in Taiwan, and then helping to impart that knowledge and experience to others. When people ask me what it is exactly that I do, I struggle to answer. Country image, yes. Branding, yes. But in some ways, I suppose I see myself more expert in the Politics of National Development. That seems to be my main takeaway, and now, what I try to impart to you here.

1 BUSTING THE DEMOCRACY MYTH

Since its inception in 1776, the United States has prided itself on being God's gift to democracy. Generation after generation of American kids grow up being indoctrinated (dare I say brainwashed?) with themes centered on American exceptionalism and global leadership based on our unrivaled freedom and *so-called* democratic heritage.

In the 20th Century, the Soviet Union also made similar claims. Its Constitution asserted the same unassailable and inalienable rights as that of the U.S. The Soviets asserted supremacy in terms of their workers' paradise, a utopia in the works. I know all about it because I had the rare opportunity to study in the former Soviet Union. I read the Soviet Constitution is Russian. I read and listened to all their state propaganda in Russian. There was very little left to the imagination. The Soviets were claiming to be a mirror image of the U.S. in terms of freedom and democracy, except with the additional assertion that their communist economic system gave them a higher purpose and superiority over the Western democracies. Orwell could not have written a better script for the Soviet propaganda machine.

So, which of the two nations is guilty of propagating a Big Lie? Conventional wisdom clearly says the Soviet Lie was the Big Lie of the century. But what about American claims to having been a democracy since its inception? Is that not a Big Lie as well? And though its consequences may not be as frightful as its Soviet counterpart, does that make it any less excusable, at least intellectually speaking?

Sure it was a lie. The United States was not a true democracy in its first 150 years of existence. It was authoritarian. Let's consider the common definition of that term: "rule by a subclass of individuals who elect or otherwise anoint themselves or their representatives to rule over the whole." That could be a strongman ruler, a military junta, or a system of one-Party rule, as in China today. Or it could be a class of individuals, say, white men over the age of 21? Hmm.

In the U.S. model, until 1920, women, who made up more than 52% of the population consistently, were not allowed to participate in elections or governance. They had no say in the process. Neither did persons of "color," which included not only Blacks but also Asians and Near Easterners and so on. Prior to 1920, roughly 58 to 60 percent of the American population was barred from participating in elections and governance. That folks, is what is known as an authoritarian system. A minority class of white males were electing themselves to rule over every one else, pure and simple. While their inner circle behaved clearly within democratic principles, it does not change the fact that America was a practicing authoritarian regime. In China, for instance, the higher echelons of the Communist Party hold elections every ten years to elect the nation's leaders. Does that mean China is a democracy? Clearly not. Under the same rules of logic or definitions, neither was the U.S. for its first 150 years.

Authoritarianism is often thought to be practiced by a single leader, an ALMOST dictator. But in fact, it's critically important here to reiterate that this is not true. A collective of like individuals holding all the power meets the definition of authoritarianism as well. I reckon this is probably the first time you are hearing all this!

Back to the Soviet Lie, there is no question in my mind, or my own personal experience, that it was by far the more heinous lie. Ronald Reagan was ridiculed by left wing groups in the West when he called the Soviet Union the "Evil Empire." In fact, my experience there told me he was right on, and that as usual, the Left was deluding itself by living in some kind of hermetically sealed utopian dream world. The Soviet Union was Orwell de facto; it was a brutal totalitarian regime that had a single interest: Totally dominate the people and the life of the nation so as to perpetuate its own rule. Think Animal Farm or 1984.

Contrast that with the United States and, of course, you have nearly night and day situations. I am not arguing that the U.S. is currently NOT a democracy. Rather, I am simply arguing that we have our own historical lies, and while they may be dwarfed by what the Soviets were putting forth, the fact remains that we have deluded ourselves about our democracy from the start, and for long enough.

Now, you might ask, what does it matter? The result is good, so who cares? Well, think Egypt. We have the domineering USA bearing down on them, trying to force that nation once again to put democracy ahead of overall economic development. It matters because our own development model was nothing like that. We put economics first for more than 150 years before transitioning to a full-blown democracy. Why impose our Big Lie or self-delusions on Egyptians, or anyone else, for that matter? Why not try the truth, and give the Egyptians a fighting chance at long-term prosperity?

The issue of giving democracy a backseat to economics certainly rings true in America's own history. Let's try this on for size: The first line of the Declaration of Independence says, "We hold these truths to be self-evident, that all men are created equal in the eyes of their Creator." Except, of course, Blacks, peoples of color and women. That means Indians, American or Indian Indian, or Hispanics, or whoever was not a white male! American children have this rammed down their throats as though it is a self-evident truth, when in fact, it was clearly a bogus assertion, when measured against what was actually being implemented or practiced. More like a goal than a statement of fact is how it should have been portrayed or interpreted. But then, why didn't the Founding Fathers just say it that way? Apologists have historically argued that the Founders could not be faulted because it was "the way it was back then." What, that women and Blacks were not people? Not humans? Beasts of burden?

I don't think so. I don't think that is what those few great minds were intending to promulgate for perpetuity. The real answer lies in the economics of the day. Nearly all the Founding Fathers, with the most notable exception of John Adams, were plantation owners. They were employing slave labor 'back then," and women, as it were, were also not much more than beasts of burden responsible for an endless cycle of daily chores, child rearing and managing the household. Neither they nor the slaves could possibly be trusted with governance off the plantation. So, I would argue that it was purely for economic reasons, and higher aspirational purposes that the Founders wrote the Declaration and later the Constitution the way they did. They were reflecting the economic realities of the day. At least I sure hope they were not a bunch of nutcases who actually thought Blacks and women were inhuman beasts of burden! I don't care when it was!

By focusing on the economics of the day, that is where their approach becomes entirely defensible. It's not defensible to argue that women and Blacks were not humans; but the history of human development clearly shows that it is defensible to argue the economics of the case for excluding "those less capable of governing" in the early stages of national development, in the context, of course, of their day.

Let's get to a key point about this book, right here.

Perhaps the single most important driving force of human development is economics, especially when it is viewed against the backdrop of governance. Mankind desires freedom and prosperity, neither of which is attainable without sound, incubative economic policies. It's all about raising living standards, constantly. People want to live better lives, and good governments want to help facilitate that aspiration, partly as a means of remaining popular and perhaps staying in power. Or, perhaps so that the noble goal of a democracy can be reached safely and soundly.

In that context, it is clear that the Founders felt they could not trust the broad population with governance. The country was dirt poor in the late 1700s. To implement full democracy would mean to risk undermining the nation's economic foundations, thereby inviting an endless cycle of uprisings and instability, and vice versa. And so it was that the economically powerful, highly educated class of white males in early America decided to keep political power close to their chests until such time that the interests of the broad population were more aligned with those of the ruling class. It was unthinkable that the masses could have the vote when they could not be trusted to understand the national interest.

That time would come on the heels of the spectacular rise of America's middle class in the early 20th Century. Hence women were granted political participation in 1920.

It was not until 1965 or so that persons of "color," particularly Blacks in America, were fully permitted to participate in the democratic process and governance. Prior to that, such obstacles to participation as literacy tests and non-institutional forms of intimidation were employed to keep them out of the process. Viewed from the perspective of our Founders, literacy tests are also defensible. The ruling class did not dare share power with the uneducated underclass, be it former slaves or poor whites, or women who had no high school or college educations. That could mean upsetting the apple cart of the economic order. Certainly unthinkable, until such a time that they could be trusted to have more aligned interests with the ruling class.

By putting economic interests ahead of true democracy, the Founders did the right thing. They took the right path. The early authoritarian rule created the conditions that were conducive to building a successful economy, one that eventually led to the creation of a massive middle class, unprecedented in human development. It's how we got to become the stable democracy we are today, and we should not shy away from simply admitting it, and actually, gloating about it.

A look back at the evolution of the American economy is quite revealing, specially as it relates to each of the stages of our gradual democratic development. By the 1870s, the Industrial Revolution was in full swing. We were moving quickly from an agrarian based economy to an industrial one, which meant a new category of jobs and paths to prosperity for the average man. Prosperity was growing exponentially, and even though there were large influxes of newcomers into the next century, the U.S. was becoming rock solid stable in political terms. By 1920, the white males congregated and decided that after nearly 150 years of exclusion, women could now be trusted with participation in governance. It was not so much because some vocal pockets of women were arguing for the same; it was more a matter of the white males feeling secure in the notion that white women now had the same stake in stability, and therefor could be trusted to share power, or at least participate in its makeup. The Stakeholder Society phase had been reached, at least for women. For certain, women still had an uphill battle for equality that they are still fighting for today.

Meanwhile, and also contrary to conventional historical narratives on democracy, other Western nations, and Japan, were following suit. Their monarchies, which had ruled over "democratically elected bodies" for centuries, were finally starting to give way to fuller democratic participation and control. By the end of WWII, most of them would see the monarchs become more like figureheads of state, rather than absolute rulers. But the evolution toward this end in Europe occurred for the exact same reason as that in the U.S.—the governing class gradually opened up to power sharing, and they became more fuller democracies secure in the notion that the "other classes" could now be trusted with governance and had interests aligned with and committed to the nation's overall stability.

If all this seems awfully simplified, don't worry, it is. No need to pile on cerebral weights or academic dullness here. My style is to keep it simple and keep it real. Just lay out the basics, and let you decide.

In sum, perpetuating the democracy first myth is not only to perpetuate a Big Lie, as it relates to the truth about our own national development, but more importantly it can cause untold harm to the developing nations that we try to bully into putting democracy first. Would it not be more sane to expect others to follow our model, our real model and not the make believe delusional one, not some dream world Big Lie? Call a spade a spade, and get on with propagating policies and conditions that reflect economic realities in developing countries first, and TEACH that once the nation is prosperous and stable, democracy COMES NATURALLY.

As was pointed out in the Foreword above, there are good models out there worth emulating. It may not be that the U.S. or any Western model is best. In fact, I will argue below that there are far more relevant models to learn from. These are models that also put economics first, but DON'T LIE ABOUT IT and certainly are not ashamed about how they developed.

2 THE RISE OF THE ASIAN TIGERS

The spectacular rise of Japan and the four Asian tigers (Taiwan, Singapore, Korea and Hong Kong) in the post-world war era is well known to most informed readers. It has also not gone unnoticed in other parts of our Solar System.

The other day I was walking in the woods down by my creek in Tippecanoe when I came across a bug-eyed, three-fingered, cone-headed alien. He introduced himself as Kryptuzyte Muchtizema (sorry, that's the best Romanization I can muster) and said he was sent from Neptune to study human development on earth. He had come to earth to figure out earthlings' overall development, and started to tell me about his key findings. No surprise here. KM said that what first caught his eye was the difference between East Asia and Latin America. Latin America was full of functioning democracies with long histories. It is also full of mostly dirt poor people. On the other hand, East Asia has the four tigers, who are new democracies (with the clear exception of Hong Kong, which is far from it), but who are amazingly rich. KM made the only intergalactic conclusion available to him: Those humans who put democracy first are dirt poor, while those who put economics first are rich, and oddly enough, now democratic.

Why does it take someone from Neptune to grasp this human condition? Why haven't other earthlings learned more from the four tigers? The Latins and others have had the same amount of time on earth to become prosperous. Why haven't they? Together, the four tigers' average per capita GDP income is 4.5 times higher than the average in Latin America ($33,750 vs. $7,500 according to IMF sources in 2012). What gives? Could putting democracy first be one of the chief culprits of this disparity?

Add to this the fact that the developmental patterns of the four tigers were not cryptic at all. They are plain to see, and have unmistakable lessons, even for an alien visitor. The tigers all went through highly accelerated stages of economic development. They basically achieved in 25 years what it took Western nations 125 years to do. Next, with the exception of HK, they went through long periods of democratic tutelage, starting at the grassroots level and working their way up, transitioning to full democracy also in a relatively short period of time (proving, also, the correlation between economic prosperity and democratic development). Granted, the tigers were dealing with relatively smaller populations, with Singapore and Hong Kong functioning like city-states. But Taiwan (23 million) and Korea (55 million) were nothing to sneeze at in terms of size.

Let's run through the basics.

The first thing the tigers had in common was authoritarian rule. But these were not your run-of-the-mill banana republic strongmen. They were enlightened, open and heavily influenced by the West. Taiwan's brand of authoritarian rule started out with Chiang Kai-shek as an individual but later evolved into one-Party rule with the Nationalists, or KMT, in charge. In Singapore, it was the much heralded statesman Lee Kuan-yew, who ruled that city-state for decades. In South Korea, it started with the strong man authoritarian rule of Syngmen Rhee, giving way to the Parks and then to a ruling party. In Hong Kong, for goodness sakes, you had the least democratic piece of real estate on the planet, since it was a full-blown colony of Britain! In Japan, which led the way for the four tigers, power had gradually shifted from an authoritarian monarchy to that of a solidly entrenched ruling party for decades (the LDP). Either way, the ruling class in Japan could be defined as authoritarian, right up until the nation reached the Stakeholder Society milestone, and evolved into a full-fledged democracy into the Seventies.

The second thing the four tigers had in common was a clear Social Compact between the governors and the governed. In Taiwan's case, which we will go into much more detail on in a later chapter, Generalissimo Chiang Kai-shek struck a deal with the Taiwan Chinese in early 1950. He promised his regime would be all about delivering freedom and prosperity, eventually getting around to democracy, according to a national development plan first laid out by Dr. Sun Yat-sen, the founder of the

Republic of China (the National Government apparatus that fled to Taiwan following the Communist take over of Mainland China in 1949). The broad base of Taiwan Chinese bought into this Social Compact.

In Singapore, Korea and HK, the same type of Social Compact existed. In exchange for restrictions on civil liberties and certain political and security controls, the governments would deliver freedom and prosperity through a series of planned economic policies and stages of development. In all cases, the folks bought into the deal.

The Social Compacts of the four tigers laid the foundation for the long-term stability of their respective societies. This was a critical step toward implementing well-planned out stages of economic development, constantly moving toward the goal of delivering prosperity and better lives. All four tigers achieved economic growth rates consistently above ten percent for a period of 25 to 30 years. That's how it is done. In all but HK's case, it also meant delivering on the promise of eventually giving way to democratic rule, once the Stakeholder Society conditions had been met. While HK remains in a colonial form of rule (for the most part), the other three are now among the most vibrant democracies on the planet.

Once the Social Compact had worked its magic, leaders in Taiwan, Korea and Singapore all had the vision to know when the Stakeholder Society had been created and that their authoritarian rule could give way to full-democracy and multi-party politics. All three could have sat on their rule longer, but none did. By the late Eighties, multi-party politics had started to take a firm hold and by the turn of the 21st Century, all three were primed for peaceful transfers of power at the presidential level. All three made incredibly stable transitions to democracy, unlike the myriad nations that continue to struggle with violence and warfare, the curse of having taken to the democratic path or the wrong kind of authoritarian rule, without a Stakeholder Society in place first.

While the four tigers have stolen most of the limelight on this development "miracle," let's not forget that Malaysia followed right on their heels with a very similar model. Authoritarian rule led the way to economic prosperity into the Nineties and Aughts, and only then did the ruler, Mahathir, give way to democracy. He also had the vision and courage to see the Social Compact through to a successful Stakeholder Society, which then evolved into full-blown democracy.

There are other factors important to the success of the national development models of the four tigers. Most critical is probably the existence of an open, enlightened, and highly educated class of technocrats in each country who were called upon to be ministers in the Cabinets of the authoritarian leader. Chiang Kai-shek started this in 1950 in Taiwan when he surrounded himself with the cream of China's crop of development brains. A troika is most notable, composed of Chen Cheng, then governor of Taiwan Province, K.T. Li, who would come up with the idea for Taiwan's famous land reform, and Sun Yun-suan, an engineer by trade who would have the president's ear on national planning and infrastructural issues. Another who played a critical role on the banking side was Yu Kuo-hwa.

As the years went by, Chiang installed ministers who were largely Ph.D.s from the US, Great Britain and Germany. The emphasis put on technocratic rule cannot be overestimated. The results were stunning. But it required an open and enlightened leader to go down this path of development.

In Korea and Singapore, ditto. The authoritarian states enlisted not only the services but also the buy-in of highly qualified technocrats who then assisted with mapping out and implementing the stunning national development that occurred in each of these states.

Hong Kong, meanwhile, was being governed by the British just fine. ALL the emphasis was on prosperity and an unrivaled environment of market freedoms and openness. Despite being a colony, Hong Kong had become synonymous with free markets and free ports. It became Asia's top financial center due to its unparalleled freedoms of capital movement, low taxes and many other market incentives. Hong Kong never needed to be a technocracy like the other tigers because it had very little territory to develop. Instead, the British made it into a world port, a world financial center, requiring little in the way of infrastructure, but with Big Business and sound British governing institutions definitely at the helm.

Hong Kong is also demonstrative when it comes to the natural evolution of democracy following achievement of the Stakeholder Society. While Hong Kong is an economic success story, and has long since passed the point of having a Stakeholder Society, it continues to suffer the fate of something akin to colonialism, as it is now formally part of China. That means it has NOT been free to develop the democracy that it has earned. Instead, it still sails along mainly committed to the stability needed to keep the economy roaring ahead, but along the way it is beginning to also show signs of unrest over the democracy issue. Hong Kong is proving out the notion that once things are rosy economically and the vast majority of the folks have a vested interest in stability, then the next aspiration on their plate is usually political participation. Hong Kong, being neither here nor there in terms of its political structure, will continue to wrestle over its model. Back when Britain was preparing to hand Hong Kong back to China in 1999, friends in the USA often asked me what would happen to Hong Kong. I argued that the only thing that would change is the flag. While many thought Hong Kong would collapse or be mismanaged under Communist rule, I didn't believe it for a second. For starters, the Stakeholder element was too deeply embedded in the minds and affairs of the Hong Kong Chinese. They would not risk losing the fruits of their decades of hard work in building Hong Kong into a world financial powerhouse. Moreover, the Communist Chinese also had every reason to maintain Hong Kong as it had been. The old story about killing the Golden Goose became popular in much of the discourse about Hong Kong's future, and it has proven to be correct. Not only did China have no interest in destroying Hong Kong (specially since at the time it was responsible for most of the outside investment fueling China's own dramatic industrialization—before Taiwan took over that role by the end of the Nineties), but China also knew that it was embarking on a four tiger-like path of development of its own, and it would not be in in its national interests to undermine Hong Kong in any way. In any case, Hong Kong remains very instructive on the difference between freedom and democracy, and how economic success, and for that matter overall development success, depends entirely on the former and not the latter. In terms of its political development, Hong Kong remains in a no-man's land, unable to move on to the natural next stage of development (democracy) but unwilling to risk what it has to fight for that right. Hmmm. Makes one think, don't it?

Another feature of the four tigers success was their emphasis on education. All four had committed to paths of development that would spawn not only rapid growth but also egalitarian growth in terms of distribution of wealth and the elimination of poverty. Indeed, Taiwan is the world's best example of rapid but egalitarian growth. It eliminated poverty completely in a short 25 years! It reached the Turning Point of economic development faster than any place on earth.

But it did so partly as a result of an education system that was designed to make the working class the middle class. Those who did not pass the strict college entrance exams could opt for technical schools in which English and technical skills were combined. This laid the foundation for Taiwan's later stage of export development.

The other tigers did the same thing. Call it a Confucian influence if you want (emphasis on education to raise up the individual), but it was more a consideration of economic planning than anything else at the time. The importance of education in the success of the tigers cannot be overlooked. In most failed models around the globe, you will find horrible neglect of public education. It is a very telling contrast, and one that our bug-eyed alien buddy KM picked up on as well.

Next on the list of what the four tigers did right is fiscal conservatism. Unlike most developing countries, who are shackled by welfare states, the four tigers resisted the temptation to give into the less productive Social Compact that revolves around delivery of a welfare state to placate the folks. Rather than go that route, like most of Latin America and Africa has, the four tigers created the incentives for people to pursue happiness through economic prosperity. Economic policies were fully designed to unleash the power of the individual and entrepreneurs in particular, while also providing the means for the working class to improve its lot. Sort of like a "no person left behind" environment.

Admittedly, the four tigers had one thing they could rely on to avoid the need for a welfare state: the strong family unit typical of Confucian cultures. Families would take care of those potentially left behind, not the state. Welfare is anathema to the Confucian culture that has long permeated the national lives of people in East Asia. This is vastly different from the expectation in say, Latin America, where national budgets are terribly burdened by spending on welfare.

But fiscal conservatism in terms of avoiding the welfare state is only one piece of the equation the tigers called upon. Equally important was their emphasis on conservative government spending on infrastructure in the early days of development. Each of the leaders seemed to have an inherent recognition that when the government coffers began to pile up with riches, they had to show restraint on spending until the time was right for the right kinds of investment in national infrastructure. And, they also timed development projects for their next stage of national development, with great timing at almost every juncture.

Again, Taiwan led the way. By the late 1970s, President Chiang Ching-kuo had decided that the time was ripe and the coffers were full enough for a bold set of infrastructural projects that would propel the island through its next 25 years of development. He launched the Ten Major Projects in 1977. More on this later…

On spending, Taiwan and Korea had a bad disadvantage: Each was faced with an overwhelming security threat and was obliged to spend as much as forty percent of their national budgets on defense. Taiwan was fending off the Communist Mainland of China while South Korea faced off with the unpredictable and massively armed North. Just think. If it were not for these huge budgets dedicated to defense spending over a period of four or five decades, what more could the Taiwanese and Koreans have added to their economic development miracles??

A final factor worth mentioning here was the four tigers' comparative lack of corruption at any level of government. Corruption, of course, exists everywhere, even in the mature, rule of law democracies. But unlike their counterparts in say Africa or Latin America, the four tigers were relatively corruption free. That is probably an understatement. This matters tremendously in national development, specially if an authoritarian system is in place. If corruption sets in in the authoritarian model, you end up dirt poor and the strongman and his cronies zap the country blind of its resources and wealth. This occurs over and over again in Africa and in Latin America. In Africa, it is reported that corruption steals away as much as ninety cents out of every dollar intended for development. Dictators end up enriching themselves until they are overthrown by the next dictator who repeats the pattern and so on. It's a long line of wannabe dictators waiting at the trough.

In Latin America, ironically, corruption permeates democracies with no end in sight. The system is such that the current president spends four years enriching himself and his cronies, only to be followed by the next democratically elected president who does the same. Wannabe leaders actually wait in line for their "turns" in some cases, with back room deals on who gets to go next. Corruption trumps national development, and the result is that Latin American countries continue to wallow in poverty and continue to disappoint. It's bad enough that they swallow the Democracy Drug in the first place, or are too accepting of the bad sort of authoritarian strongman at the other end of the spectrum. But corruption certainly worsens things beyond repair, in most cases.

The four tigers were never burdened with such unpleasantries. Nothing trumped collective national development. Ever.

These are the main set of factors that fueled the stunning economic and political successes of the four tigers (with HK excepted, once again, on politics).

It's at this point that I want to share with you what I think is the most important statement of policy on national development ever made. It came from President Chiang Ching-kuo in Taiwan in 1978, when he took over the presidency from C.K. Yen. He declared that Taiwan would continue on its course of seeking "STABILITY WITH PROGRESS, AND PROGRESS WITH STABILITY."

That really sums up the most critical ingredient for successful national development. The records of Taiwan and the other tigers show us that a nation MUST remain stable in both social and political terms for at least 25 years in order for sound economic policies aimed at creating prosperity and ending poverty to run their course. AND, lo and behold the other prize at the end of the rainbow is democracy! But Chiang was iterating that without stability, there would be no progress. And conversely, if the government could not provide progress, there would be no stability. Hence the Social Compact. The most important takeaway for national leaders who stumble upon this book is this one from Chiang Ching-kuo. Every nation, whatever its culture and status, can learn from this greatest of all admonitions on the fundamental requirements for national development. If Egypt is to have any rational hope at all, it must learn this lesson.

3 THE PHILIPPINES: AN AUGHTA BE TIGER LOSES ITS WAY

I am not an expert on The Philippines. No pretenses here. But I do know this one awful thing about The Philippines: It had all the ingredients in place to become a fifth tiger, if not the strongest of all tigers, given its larger size and availability of resources, both human and natural, compared to its four neighbors who went on to stunning national development success. Not to mention it also had the full support of the United States, culturally, militarily and economically. Indeed, The Philippines had a certain affinity with the U.S. that the other tigers did not measure up to.

But none of it would matter. The Philippines became like the fifth Beatle instead of the fifth tiger—largely forgotten and written off as a basket case, even to this day.

And that is doubly disappointing for this reason: The Philippines, a 100 years ago, was actually one of the richest countries in Asia! It had a tremendous head start on everyone else!

What went wrong? How could the one nation in Asia with the closest ties to the U.S. be the one that failed us most? With a pitiful per capita GDP of $2,617 in 2012, The Philippines is an example of failed U.S. intervention and toleration of the wrong kind of authoritarian rule over a long period of time.

It is really quite simple, especially when viewed against the backdrop of what transpired in the other tigers. The Philippines let its authoritarian rule evolve into a bad form that put the interests of the leader ahead of those of the nation. In other words, Manila had the wrong kind of authoritarian rule. The wrong kind of strongman.

President Ferdinand Marcos, his wife and his tight circle of cronies used the levers of power to enrich themselves at the expense of national development. Unlike the Lees in Singapore, the Chiangs in Taiwan and the Parks in Korea, Marcos went on a three-decade narcissistic binge in which little to no economic development occurred and political power would be selfishly guarded. If the term Banana republic is still relevant, then The Philippines is definitely a hall of famer in that class. Maybe it came partially from its Latin roots. But I would bet it has more to do with the influence of Marcos in creating an entire system of corruption that became entrenched not only institutionally, but also in the national psyche. Bottom line, he screwed his country big time. The wrong kind of strongmen can actually do that.

Marcos zapped the country's resources in two ways.

First, nearly everything was meant for his own enrichment or for that of his inner circle of family friends. Second, with the country constantly wallowing in an abject state of poverty and economic and political corruption, it experienced a severe brain drain. The best Filipinos took flight to the USA or Southeast Asian nations. Because of their native English skills, they could find really good jobs with advertising firms, design firms, PR firms and so on. Any time a nation suffers this kind of brain drain it severely hampers national development. For his part, Marcos was probably happy to see them all go. Less people to crack down on, less potential political competition from the nation's intellectuals.

The U.S. tolerated Marcos because of the crucial role The Philippines played in the security picture in East Asia. The U.S. had two major bases there, the Subic Bay Naval Base and the Clark Air Force Base, both outside Manila. The U.S. dominated the economic activity that did take place in and around Manila well into the Nineties, but that dissipated with the closing of the bases after Marcos fell from power.

Which brings us to the important irony of The Philippines: It did not take off like the other tigers because it had the wrong brand of authoritarian rule. It went nowhere under Marcos. But, after Marcos fell and democracy was instantly implemented, the nation still has gone nowhere. The new reason? Because it's democratic. It took the ass-backward Western Big Lie approach. Instead of learning from its neighbors, which completely surround it, The Philippines has put democratic pride ahead of rational thinking on national development.

Democracy never works in the early stages of development, and The Philippines provides important clues as to why that is so. First, when you suddenly go from a long era of strongman rule (the bad kind) to a democratically elected president and a real parliament, all hell breaks loose with competing interests fighting for their share of the former pie dominated in this case, by the Marcos family. It may be that the Aquinos who took power after Marcos were clean (and they probably were by most accounts), but they could not govern effectively because the society had gone from singular control to out of control competition for financial, political and other interests. This form of instant democracy breeds a massive rise of self-interests, but instead of serving the whims of a single self-interested party or person, now everyone is competing against each other, and lo and behold, the nation's collective interests are lost in the turmoil. You are back where you started.

Second, The Philippines is far too poor to endure this unstable political environment. What's truly needed is an authoritarian ruler or party with the same technocratic focus as the tigers had. Only then could the nation lift itself out of poverty and rise like its neighbors around it. The Philippines desperately needs 25 straight years of well-planned economic development. It needs an open, enlightened authoritarian structure to make that happen. There is no other way to create the conditions for annual growth rates of 10% over 25 years, so that the nation can overcome poverty and rise to the level of its East Asian neighbors. On its present course, The Philippines will be mired in horrible poverty, well, perpetually.

Unfortunately, that does seem to be the likely outcome. Though it sits smack dab in the tigers' den, The Philippines has embarked on a path of national development that is more akin to that of its ancestral cousins in Latin America. Put democracy first, remain poor.

A trip to Manila leaves one bewildered. U.S. influence is quite evident in much of the trappings of the society, but with the exception of the prosperity enjoyed by the top two percent, the rest of the city, and the country for that matter (with the exception of some nice beaches in the south!) is dirt poor and disgustingly so. Why? Because it just should not be. The Philippines is one big disappointment.

The lack of a clearly defined social compact, and the lack of enlightened, open authoritarian rule, is going to continue to keep this nation not only down, but also faced with insurgencies from sectors of the society that see no hope. When half out of every dollar of development money disappears (according to friends in Manila), there can be no hope. Government, as it currently resides in Manila, simply cannot be expected to deliver the promise of prosperity. The Philippines will continue to be the red-headed step child of East Asia…

4 BACKING THE STRONGMAN: THE DEVILS YOU KNOW SYNDROME

In the first half of my fifty odd years, the world was dominated by the Cold War, which featured competition between the Soviet bloc and the U.S. sphere of influence around the globe. The world was not only divided into Communist and non-Communist blocs , but was also the arena for much competition between the U.S., the Soviet Union and Communist China *within* developing nations. In Latin America, Africa, Southeast Asia and the Middle East civil wars and conflicts were often proxy wars between the superpowers, leaving behind a trail of disaster, a vicious circle of war, revolution, poverty and disease. Certainly no economic development. In most cases, it was a matter of supporting one devil you know (the right wing strongman) versus the other devil you know as well (the Communist-backed strongman). It was never a case of the devil we knew versus the devil we did not know, as the commonly used notion goes. One is reminded of the tough choice the U.S. had to make in W.W. II when it came to back one ruthless, mass murder (Stalin) over another (Hitler). History is replete with such choices being foisted on nations, who end up choosing one over the other on the basis of the more immediate national interest, or at least, in attempt to side with the winner.

This competition forced the U.S. into unholy alignments with so-called right-wing dictatorships and other otherwise unseemly authoritarian regimes that happened to be aligned with U.S. military interests first, and perhaps a smidgen of economic interests here and there. Continents were divided as a result. Africa, for instance, had a handful of Soviet satellites, a handful aligned with Communist China and the rest still hanging in there with strong European ties or emerging ties with the U.S. Latin America was also fertile ground for Cold War competition for influence, as was Southeast Asia.

To fend off Soviet interests, the U.S. invariably found itself backing such right-wing strongmen or authoritarian regimes around the globe. Though most of these were undesirables when viewed against the backdrop of the human rights tradition in the U.S. and West, Washington nevertheless had to rely on these relationships to deter or offset Soviet influence. Such regimes also included Taiwan, Korea and Singapore, who were playing frontline roles in the face-off with Communism. These, as we have argued above, were the class of "desirable authoritarianism," and are not included in the current discussion on strongman rule.

In terms of geo-politics, the backing of strongman rule,

so long as the strongman was pro-U.S., was arguably justified. This "devil you know versus the other devil you know," or "communism versus freedom and democracy," was the seeming constant factor in many of these civil conflicts. For the U.S., it was a key means of stunting the combined growth of Soviet and Chinese Communist influence around the globe. But many of these alliances were constantly contested at home, with America's Left always harping about the hypocrisy of dealing so closely with such strongmen regimes, even if they were the "enemies of my enemy." And, even if the Communists had a much more brutal record of rule.

The subject of U.S. support for strongman regimes over the past fifty years, and likewise Soviet and Chinese Communist support for regimes on their side of the ideological divide, has important ramifications for any review of the role democracy, and the right kind of authoritarianism, plays in national development. Indeed, even a cursory look at the body of evidence is illuminating. Neither side is guilt-free. The Soviets openly stated their ambition to unite the world under Communist rule. But rather than moving offensively to cultivate freedom and sound economic policies in our client proxy war states, the U.S. opted instead to merely take a more militaristic defensive stance, most often ignoring what our strong men "partners" were doing at home.

One of the earliest and best examples of "satellite" strongman rule occurred on the Soviet side—Cuba. When Castro took power following a brief revolution in 1959, the U.S. was largely caught off guard. Suddenly, it had a

Soviet satellite right on its own doorstep. That was alarming not only for military reasons, giving the Soviets such close proximity to U.S. shores, but also in terms of Cuba's potential for spreading the "revolutionary communist disease" throughout the region.

As it turned out, Cuba became the poster child for Soviet bloc satellite regimes. It mirrored the Soviet gulag politically, while seeking to implement a communist economic system. Castro became a dictator, and he alone ruled over nearly every aspect of Cuban life. Along the way, Cuba has remained one of the poorest nations on earth, certainly a big under-performer given its true economic potential, which has been suppressed for sixty years now. With the Castros slowly beginning to make their exit from the scene (due to natural causes!), there is more and more talk about what Cuba will look like in the post-Castro era. My view is that other countries in the Caribbean need to be concerned, but for a good reason: Cuba is going to explode on the scene when it opens up. There will be a great sucking sound in the Caribbean—the sound of foreign investment and tourism going to Cuba! All the smaller, nearby nations, particularly Jamaica, will have to prepare for this eventuality. Cuba, when it is left to its natural capitalist inclinations, will become a powerhouse economy. But first, it will need a new leadership, soft-authoritarian in nature, to lead the nation to a new economic reality. Ironically, Cuba can learn nothing from its former Russian mentor; instead, they would be better served taking their cues from China., if they are to successfully make the transition from communist to break-neck capitalism and free markets.

On the U.S. side of the equation, the relationship with Iran in the Sixties and Seventies is worth examining. Largely propped up by U.S. military and other levers of support, the Shah of Iran was considered one of America's firmest allies. But his ruling style did not always sit well with human rights groups in the U.S. and Europe. The regime was under constant criticism. But because the geo-political stakes were so high in such a volatile region of the world, the U.S. hung in there with the Shah.

The deposing of the Shah in 1979 by Islamic fanatics took the U.S. off guard (once again!). The ayatollah-led revolt happened quickly and it was all the U.S. could do but to rescue the Shah at the last minute and provide him with asylum.

Where did the Shah go wrong? Iran had long been a progressing, technocratic society, with hundreds of thousands of Iranian students studying and working in the U.S. Back in the Seventies, Iran was second only to Taiwan in terms of the number of students in U.S. graduate schools.

But the Shah, like Marcos in The Philippines, simply could not get beyond the powerful levers of rule that he had used to maintain his power. He relied on brutal methods to suppress any opposition. That is one thing. The other is that he did not implement technocratic shared rule, or an effective national economic development plan, that could keep up with the aspirations of the people, especially the young people. In other words, he failed to deliver on any Social Compact that may or may not have been implicit in his rule. Iranians saw no light at the end of the Shah's tunnel, and he was toppled.

The U.S., as we will see in many examples in Latin America, was also complicit in the Shah's failures. At no time did the U.S. insist on implementation of anything remotely like a social compact that the Iranian people could have bought into. Rather than promote socio-economic policies that could be conducive to achieving progress in national development, and soothing the folks' economic aspirations, the U.S. let the Shah do it his way and his way alone.

The problem is, what came next has turned out to be far worse for the Iranian people. Rather than liberators as promised, the ayatollahs quickly turned Iran into one of the least free places on earth. It is an Islamist version of the Soviet gulag. Once again, young people are getting restless, and starting to turn against the regime. That is natural, but this time, more attention will need to be paid to the outcome. Anyone who thinks democracy is the answer is dead wrong. Iran needs something very different if it is to prosper and grow with stability. Iran needs a leader who will rise up, espouse the virtues of a strong Social Compact, and lay out a plan for aggressively marching toward prosperity, with democracy as the ultimate fruit of those efforts. The U.S. would need to come out of its own democratic stupor and wake up to the realities of how national development really occurs.

In hindsight, the U.S. should have pressed upon the Shah from the beginning a series of national plans that would take the country through to a Stakeholder Society. Instead of merely backing a strongman who acted as a major pivot foot for the U.S. in the Middle East, the U.S. should have insisted on a much broader package of conditions for backing him. During those years we were doing such things in Korea and Taiwan and Singapore. Why not in Iran?

The answer probably lies in the degree of fear the U.S. had over the Middle East. It was willing to partner with any "enemy of my enemy" no matter how unseemly the ruler was. Nearly all of the Arab regimes are also authoritarian, ruled by family monarchies with tight controls over their respective societies, and certainly with tight fisted political control. This has been deemed to be either a cultural thing or a "necessary evil" in keeping the delicate balances of power in the region. We'll talk more about the current Arab Spring phenomenon later…

In Latin America, the Cold War conflict was played out time and again. The U.S. backed authoritarian rulers in Panama, Nicaragua, Chile and elsewhere, offsetting the advance of left-wing regimes with Soviet ties throughout the Seventies and into the Eighties.

The derogatory term "banana republic" came out of the Latin American experience. And for good reason. The continent has been dominated by regimes that are either straight up authoritarian (the bad kind) or those strangled by abused democracy. Latins like to say they have long democratic histories, but that it quickly proven delusional with a cursory glance at the political history of the continent. More often than not, since their independence was by and large gained in the 1820s, Latin countries have been ruled by oligarchies (families), military juntas and dictators.

Chile provides a very interesting test case. When Salvador Allende was president in the late Sixties and into early Seventies, he was surrounded by Soviet KGB advisors and was moving to align himself and the country completely with Soviet interests. The U.S. countered with CIA efforts and economic sanctions to undermine him. Soon, the country tanked and the military removed Allende in 1973. His successor was the Supreme Military Commander, Augusto Pinochet, who was backed by the U.S. He immediately moved to the common model of Latin American dictator. He brutally suppressed his opposition. He did, however, take an unusual approach in terms of economics. He surrounded himself with technocrats and Big Business types, a group of technocrats known as the Chicago Boys (named after their ties to the University of Chicago School of Business). While he maintained an iron fist on the politics of the nation, Chile actually began to grow enormously in economic terms. It became the darling of the West. The U.S. certainly backed him. Chileans ended up divided over his rule, with many still arguing that the economic progress was not worth the cost of the political stranglehold over the nation. Pinochet was eventually ousted, but it wasn't until decades later that the irony of his rule really began to emerge. Since around 2004, there has been a sort of nostalgia taking root in Chile over Pinochet's rule. With Chile's economy having been mainly stagnant for thirty years, people were starting to reminisce about the, uh, "good 'ol days" of a booming economy under Pinochet.

In my work for Colombia in 2004-2007, I happened to have interviewed tens of Chilean business people on this subject. A nostalgic view was definitely taking hold among the business class, and for good reason. They had come around to understand that authoritarian rule could have its good side. There has been an increasing view that while Pinochet did much harm to the country politically, and that the human toll of rule was high, his economic policies were quite another story.

The problem with Pinochet, however, goes back to the Shah of Iran example. His brutal political tactics undermined, rather than contributed to, the nation's overall stability. He was constantly facing unrest at home. He simply did not go far enough in trying to establish a more stable Social Compact that could have alleviated or even precluded the constant political unrest. Instead, his brutal suppression tactics helped foment more unrest. In hindsight, it now seems that many Chileans would have bought into such a compact, for the sake of not only stability but also for the economic progress it would have brought, on top of what was already occurring in a *less* stable environment.

Since Pinochet, Chile has been a democracy. It has fared okay, but nowhere near to its potential. It has tremendous resources, resourceful people and knows how to promote itself. But, in the overall scheme of things, it remains dirt poor and has been stagnant of late. To overcome poverty and take its place among the developed nations of the world, Chile needs something different. It needs 20 years of authoritarian rule.

In every other case in Latin America where the U.S. backed the wrong kind of right-wing strongman, the country has failed to achieve economic progress. This is a shame. The U.S. could have pressed upon the strongmen rulers a set of rules more akin to what Taiwan and Korea were doing, rather than just letting these regimes off the hook because they were, geo-politically speaking, the "enemies of my enemy." Central America, where more of the U.S. backed authoritarian regimes were located, remains mired in poverty, for two reasons.

First, some of them still have strongman rule and have not budged from that model. These are the poorest of the poor. Second, and again ironically, the ones who have implemented democracy are, while slightly better off, still wallowing in poverty and systems in which the two percent have all the power (politically and economically) over society.

Democratically speaking, the most successful regime in Central America is Costa Rica. It has balanced democracy with enlightened economic policies perhaps better than any other nation in the region. Yet, with all its resources, it remains a poor undeveloped nation. And it will stay there so long as presidents with vastly different views on national development come and go as a result of free elections.

We will examine in more detail the failure of Latin

America to deliver on economic development, and the key reasons behind that failure.

For now, let's turn our attention to the widespread culture of strongman rule in Africa. Nowhere is the outcome of the worst type of such rule more evident than in Africa.

One of the most shocking books I have ever read (on any subject) is Tom Jones's *The Broken Continent*. A long time reporter in Africa for the Economist, Jones lays out a horrifying case for why Africa has failed to deliver progress to its people (with the notable exception of South Africa).

The main takeaways from the book are that Africa suffers from two diseases: An endless stream of self-interested strongman rule, and unbelievable levels of corruption, both of which suck the continent dry of any hope for progress, decade in and decade out. Africa has been nothing more than a revolving door of terror and self-enrichment by strongman rulers.

The nations that have fared the best in Africa are those who: 1) were not Soviet or Communist Chinese satellites in the Cold War era, and 2) those who evolved more stably from their European colonial roots, rather than having undergone violent revolutions that typically led to worse conditions under native rule.

In his book, Jones, repeatedly refers to the example of Robert Mugabe's Zimbabwe. A Harvard educated technocrat, Mugabe chose to return to his native country, the former Rhodesia, which, like South Africa, had also been ruled by Whites for more than a century. Mugabe led the transition government and took power in a "democratic" election. Soon after taking power, however, the African curse set in and he turned quickly into one of the continent's most brutal dictators, still clinging to power today. Needless to say, the country is wretchedly poor and going nowhere, again despite having plenty of resources from which to grow a decent economy. Mugabe was the darling of the West when he returned home, but his total failure to deliver on economics or democracy have put him at the top of the heap of the West's least favorite dictators. In this case, democracy turned out to be a hoax, nothing more than a ruse for Mugabe to take power and keep it to this day.

A few of the biggest basket cases in Africa are countries that still cling in one form or another to their Communist bloc pasts. Most notable, I think, is Mozambique. It has a geography that is Chile-like, running more than a thousand miles down the East coast of mid-to-southern Africa, like a finger. It has tremendous natural resources, and all that shoreline. Yet, it remains one of the poorest nations in the world, largely because its rulers cannot let go of their past ties with Communism and Communist China in particular. Its people, particularly its White minority, are hugely disappointed. They can see a roadmap toward prosperity, but are perpetually denied the means to make it happen. The country simply has the wrong kind of authoritarian rulers, and that is a huge shame. I place Mozambique at the top of my list of African nations with the most potential, but to reach that potential it will need a different political structure (and by now, we know which kind!).

Most other African nations suffer from similar ills. Uganda suffered horribly under Idi Amin. The tales of his excesses are "legendary," as is the Hollywood told version of Rwanda. The Congo (now the Central African Republic), Nigeria and…Let's just stop here with any listing. It is far easier to say nearly all African nations act this way. Jones notes that Tanzania and Uganda are faring fairly well these days with more open and enlightened leaders. Ghana and Kenya, which held more true to their European roots, have long been better performers on the continent, but still continual disappointments overall. Kenya has been aligned more closely with the U.S. in recent decades, which has helped it along better than others, but it still suffers from the Democracy Drug. It needs something other than the revolving door of self-interest that comes with each national election for president.

As does South Africa, which is widely considered to be Africa's best success story. Most attribute that squarely to its former White rule (authoritarian but focused on economics—sound familiar by now?) and its history making transition from the excesses and evils of apartheid to a central government now dominated by Blacks and the African National Congress (party). The man who rightfully gets credit for the peaceful turnover of power from White to Black is Nelson Mandela. Mandela was a rare figure in world history, a Jesus-like believer in such counter-intuitive themes as "love thine enemy and former oppressor" and a visionary leader who understood that violent retribution against the old oppressors would only sink the economic progress already achieved and likely set it back for decades. Such vision is indeed rare, and I dare say it has only occurred once in all of Africa's history.

Black rule does, however have some negative influence on South Africa's overall well-being. As Jones reports, there is growing corruption and reverse favoritism in which Black owned businesses win projects even if they are less qualified to do the job. This has caused an increasingly worrisome degree of White flight, which the nation can hardly afford given the economic power these people have traditionally held. Giving way to an underclass, or less qualified privileged class, is not the answer, but it turns out South Africa may be headed in that direction. That is truly a shame. One wonders how it will evolve in the post-Mandela era…

In our review of the politics and economics of strongman rule, let's move finally to one of the most stunning examples in world history—the two Koreas. Like Mainland China and Taiwan, which we will get to in great detail in a later chapter, the two Koreas offer the most demonstrative illustration of the stark difference between "good" authoritarian rule, and its bad counterpart. Its worst counterpart, actually.

One of my favorite things to do is to look at the nighttime satellite photos of the Korean peninsula. To the north, utter darkness. Almost cave darkness! To the south, a gigantic Clifton Mill (Clifton Mill is a major, Christmas time tourism attraction east of Dayton, Ohio. It has nearly ten million lights in its display).

What the satellite photos make clear is that North Korea, under the totalitarian control of the Kim dynasty, is hands down one of the bleakest places on earth. It is Orwell on steroids, and makes the Soviet Union look like a Leninist wet dream in comparison. Not much more than a massive gulag, the entire country has been subjugated into a perpetual state of near nothingness, with mass starvations every year and nearly 90 cents out of every dollar going toward maintenance of the regime and its massive military. Arguably, North Korea has not one single good thing going for it. It is hell on earth, propped up by three things: 1) its newly acquired nuclear arsenal, 2) its massive non-nuclear military, and 3) continuing insane support from its long time benefactor, China. Had China pulled the plug just years earlier, we would be looking at an entirely different Korean Peninsula today. Instead, China's Communist rulers have opted to keep the bad boy on the planet alive though not well in their sphere. More on that later.

In contrast, South Korea is one of the world's greatest national development stories. Starting from horrific poverty levels and illiteracy levels immediately following the War in 1952, South Korea has turned itself into an economic powerhouse that now rivals the Western powers. And, lest we forget, because it also followed the Social Compact goal of reaching a Stakeholder Society, it now has a completely stable and robust democracy. The lights are on in South Korea.

Friends often get confused about the difference between totalitarian rule and authoritarian rule. First off, they naturally assume that both are bad and thus undesirable under any circumstances. But there are examples of good authoritarian rule, and the Koreas clearly prove the assumption that all are bad wrong-headed. Under a totalitarian regime, North Korea is the second or third poorest nation on earth. It is certainly the least free of all. Under authoritarian rule, however, South Korea rose to become a developed nation, a human success story only rivaled by say, Taiwan. Indeed, Taiwan and South Korea rose together, almost in tandem, and under incredibly similar conditions. They also grew according to very similar stages of development. Both faced tremendous security issues that required inordinate amounts of public spending on defense. Both had authoritarian regimes that delivered on their promise of creating near miraculous economic progress, with a focus on stability to achieve that progress. And both have emerged as stable, robust democracies at the end of the development path.

Still, there is yet another reason why Taiwan and Korea were so successful: The U.S. did not force any Democracy Drug down their throats. They were left to their own designs politically so long as they remained firm allies in the line of defending the Free World against the encroachment of Communism. Both Korea and Taiwan also paid lip service to their eventual goals of democracy, so perhaps the U.S. had reason to have faith in that promise, particularly since it was clearly part of an understood Social Compact within both countries and particularly because the U.S. knew that both Korea and

Taiwan were nurturing democracy in both their education systems and with grassroots experimentation. It was perfectly feasible for the U.S. to accept that their goals of institutionalizing democracy, eventually, were more than just lip service. That bet paid off well, for all concerned. The U.S. had no reason to meddle so long as the Koreans and Taiwan Chinese just kept on truckin' as they were.

Look at the satellite nighttime photo again. Totalitarianism to the north, the right kind of authoritarianism to the south. Simple as that. Pictures do tell a million words, don't they?

The subject of strongman rule continues to provide fodder for political debate in the West, and elsewhere for that matter. The cases of Putin in Russia and Karzi in Afghanistan come mostly to the forefront of discourse on the subject.

Detractors of U.S. support for Karzi often argue that it is morally wrong for the U.S. to support a strongman like Karzi. They say it defies U.S. democratic principles and thus hurts the cause of making any progress in that country. Parallel to this are assertions that Karzi is corrupted, and therefor not a desirable partner on that level as well.

Let's put aside the corruption issue, for now, and focus on the issue of him being a strongman. In reality, Karzi is not strong enough to lead. He does not have enough power to lead. If the U.S were going to approach Afghanistan with anything remotely resembling the Taiwan model, it should ensure that Karzi, who seems to act well enough as a bridge between his country and the outside world, and who seems to be enlightened and open for making sound economic policies, has the right kind of Social Compact in place to buy him the time he needs to get that nation's economic base on the way to development. This is a case where if most agree he is the right guy, or the lesser of any other evils, then we should equip him with the strategy for national development that is known to work. If we allow him to go off on an authoritarian tangent that is counter-productive, then he must be dealt with accordingly. Karzi needs 25 years to make what needs to happen, happen in Afghanistan.

As for Putin in Russia, well, he shows signs of being the wrong guy for the job, most of the time. For starters, his past as a diehard KGB career man is not encouraging. He is often said to be nostalgic for the good old days of the Soviet Empire. That, clearly, is in no one's interest, except perhaps a penis-envying, wannabe dictator. Second, he has a penchant for jailing and otherwise persecuting successful business people in Russia, specially those whose powers begin to either rival or at least conflict with his own. Not good. Such a disdain for the economic success of individuals is clearly a no no in any effort to create a prosperous economy. Imagine if the Parks in Korea had had the same notion and practice?

Finally, Putin shows many signs of putting his own self-interests above those of the nation. He is often in the news traveling around, living high off the hog, doing whacko things to get attention. That's another sign he would not make "our kind" of authoritarian ruler. He would not fit the bill in terms of enlightenment, openness or "softness" in his approach to leading that nation.

This harks back to a terrible mistake made by George H.W. Bush in 1989. When the Soviet regime collapsed, an open, enlightened, more Western-oriented leader emerged in Russia—Boris Yeltsin. He had led the bloodless "revolt" against the Soviet regime. In a nutshell, the world lost a real opportunity in Russia when President Bush Sr. told Yeltsin that the U.S. would not assist him economically nor in any other fashion until he had a democratically elected parliament under his belt. Yeltsin was desperate for U.S. support, and this reply could not have been worse news. It forced Yeltsin to comply, however, and what transpired is to this day very unfortunate.

By forcing the Democracy Drug down Yeltsin's and Russia's throat, the U.S. helped unleash a massive wave of pent-up self-interests in the former Soviet regime. For decades the lid had been kept on the darkest elements of Russian society, all the mob elements and others. When the lid was forced off, many of these creeps realized they could enrich themselves by running for nationally elected offices. That was one outcome of the Russian rush to democracy to meet U.S. and Western demands. The other outcome is the more normal one: A president ends up with a parliament that he cannot possibly work with because it is entirely bogged down in self-interests. There is no hope for consensus building in such an environment, and as we shall soon see in the Latin American model, the case for such a democratic institution in the early stages of development is not good at all. Nothing ever gets done, a national plan is impossible to reach, and the country stays mired in poverty because of the impotence of the democracy. Had Yeltsin been given wider powers and the right kind of leeway toward a successful brand of authoritarian rule, Russia would be a very different place today. Its people might possibly have pulled off a Taiwan or Korea style miracle. At the very least, they could have had the chance to emulate China, a model of perhaps more relevance to Russia. What a shame.

Finally, let's talk about Iraq, a country that the U.S. has put at the forefront of the global dialog on "nation-building."

Iraq is actually an embarrassing case for me to address when talking to friends around the world, particularly here in China. The reason is simple: George W. Bush would be the last person who knows anything about nation-building. While I greatly supported him in other areas, the whole Iraq thing is, well, just downright embarrassing. The U.S. has no business telling Iraq how to "nation-build." And that's mainly because we 1) ignore our own history when telling others how it's done, and 2) completely ignore the few success stories that exist (those four tigers again!).

Same 'ol same 'ol. Ram the Democracy Drug down their throats, because it looks and sounds good at home. And then sit back and watch as endless turmoil sets in and a distinct lack of progress contributes to undermining stability. The vicious circle all over again. Bush might argue that America backed Taiwan and Korea, and they succeeded, didn't they? So, it's not a matter of backing a country, it's a matter of ensuring that the country is on the right development path. And that does not mean democracy first. Especially in tribal based cultures with millennia old histories of tribal conflict, not to mention the modern day scourge of secular versus theocratic rule that now rears its ugly head throughout the Middle East.

What's needed in Iraq is something else. It may be too late to turn back the clock, but Iraq clearly needs a powerful, enlightened, open, soft authoritarian leader for two main reasons: First, it's the proven way to approach economic development, which forms the basis of all national development, including democracy down the road, and second, in Iraq's case, Arab cultures tend to be tribal and will need the right kind of strongman rule to pull together a national consensus to make prosperity happen. Unity in Iraq needs to occur as a result of shared economic progress, not through the barrel of a gun, a la Mao in Communist China. Iraq desperately needs both an authoritarian leader and a technocratic government to deliver the goods to the people. It needs a Social Compact that spells out the trade offs and goals. It must receive the people's buy-in, too.

Strongman rule did not deliver under Saddam Hussein. He siphoned much of the national GNP into his own pockets or those of his inner circle of cronies. His brutal rule was unparalleled, even in the Arab world. No thanks. Saddam was clearly the wrong kind of strongman rule.

Today, Iraq has an opportunity to implement the right kind. And for that matter, so does Egypt. As I write this, the Egyptian crisis continues to play out. There are suggestions that Mohammed ElBaradei, the former head of the U.N.'s Atomic Energy Agency, is being considered for prime minister. That is actually a good sign. At least someone understands that what Egypt needs most is technocratic leadership that will focus on real economic development as the nation's top priority. But I would go a much bigger step further. With U.S. and Western backing, I would install ElBaradei as both president and prime minister, and give him authoritarian like powers to create a Social Compact, get buy-in for it among all the competing interests in Egypt, and then let him set out to start delivering on the authoritarian technocracy's side of the bargain. This is doable in Egypt. While there will be competing religious and other interests, the people of Egypt understand the need for a new economic order, first. If they choose to follow a Taiwan or Korean model, they have the means to succeed. If they stay addicted to the Democracy Drug, they will fail. Let's hope they Just Say No to Democracy.

In conclusion here, one could come up with a Hall of Shame for Authoritarian Rulers. The list would include such losers as :

Mao Zedong

Joseph Stalin

Ho Chi Minh

But one thing is historically clear: There are two kinds of regimes holding back economic progress in the developing world. The first is the wrong kind or bad kind of authoritarian rule. The others are those who have put democracy first, and continue to wallow in mass poverty due to the inherent flaws with putting democracy first. This is where we turn our attention to the poster child continent for this latter ill, Latin America.

5 THE FAILURE OF LATIN AMERICA

As our bug-eyed buddy from Neptune quickly realized, the Latin Americans have had the same amount of time to develop prosperous societies as their East Asian counterparts. And yet, for the most part, they remain much poorer. The disparity in per capita GDP incomes, as a sheer example, are stunning. On average, the Latins have GDP per capita incomes that are one-fourth those of their four tiger counterparts. That is a pathetic outcome, and one that was certainly not necessary or accidental. Indeed, it is purely a man-made disaster.

As our alien friend had no choice but to conclude, the main reason is because the Latins put democracy first, while the East Asians put economics first. The irony is that the Asians ended up with more robust, full democracies. Rich ones, too. The East Asians got their economic pie and ate their democratic cake as well.

In November 2012, the marketing and branding magazine PM, based in Bogota, asked me to write an article detailing the challenges I faced in creating the national brand for Colombia (Colombia is Passion!). At the end of the piece, I concluded with the very negative notion that nation branding per se would be impossible to achieve over the long term in Latin America countries, mainly due to certain anomalies in their democratic systems. Specifically, I argued that it would be impossible to maintain a national brand (which by its nature is supposed to be long-term if not "forever") so long as presidents have term limits and the next guy that comes along thinks he has to change it because the existing one belongs to the former guy. This is often the case in Latin America. A new president completely rejects the agenda of his predecessor, sometimes changing course completely just to make the point of being the new guy. This pattern repeats itself over and over. It is an ego based system of top-down democracy that gives the national common good a permanent backseat to sound nation-building principles. Some countries in Latin America are totally dominated or run by egos, conflicting egos in some cases, which creates a set of conditions that are also hardly conducive to long term nation-building. During my research work in Panama, almost on a daily basis I faced a situation in which the fellow I would be interviewing would ask me whom I had just interviewed. The answer, invariably, caused the current interviewee to go into a tirade about how I wasted my time talking to a moron like that and should have just come straight to him for all the answers on Panama. This went on and on, until it seemed that every cream of the cropper in Panama considers himself to have no equals. That is taking the ego to unimaginable heights, but it is how things work in much of Latin America. To hell with the common good.

In Colombia's case, we tried to make sure that the nation brand was NOT perceived as a project of the president. We went out of our way to position it that way. But to no avail. When the then president had to step down due to term limits, the new guy quickly ended the successful nation brand and went back to square one to start one of his own. Good luck with that. We got the research right the first time. Thus we got the positioning right the first time. Anything that comes after that is just contrived, for whatever reason.

Nation branding, however, is a minor detail when contrasted with the stakes of national development in this tit-for-tat pendulum of presidential power. Changing the nation brand is nothing compared to changing the nation's development direction, all because the new guy argues that his predecessor had it all wrong. Thus, you can count on a totally zig-zag path to development in Latin democracies: National development policies change every four years or so, according to the egos that come and go at the levers of presidential power. That's insane, and completely anathema to the East Asian model where authoritarian leaders or parties stayed the course through to the Stakeholder Society and into formation of robust democracies. Latins take the slow boat zig-zag route, while the four tigers took a straight line upwards for 30 years. That's the Latin democracies. The wrong kind of authoritarian regimes have no hope for broad-based prosperity.

According to this argument, it would make sense that a nation brand could take root in the more authoritarian regimes in Latin America. That is indeed true. It would at least have a better shot at long term implementation.

Unfortunately, however, economic development in Latin America is not only hampered by a host of countries that put democracy first, but also by having exactly the wrong form of authoritarian rule. Over and over again as though there is no such thing as a learning curve in their collective national development histories. Either end of the spectrum is the wrong approach, and Latin America loves both.

A cursory glance at the history of the Continent is telling. By and large, the countries in Central and South America have been independent since the 1820s. They lay claim to having had democratic traditions since their foundings, but a look at the record suggests otherwise. Indeed, the average Latin country has been embroiled in civil war more often than not; they have been ruled by military juntas more often than not; and they have been ruled as oligarchies or strong man authoritarian regimes more often than they have actually functioned as democracies. Even when they had stable periods of what they call democracy, it really was not democracy, but more along the lines of the early U.S. model where a select minority elected or otherwise anointed itself to rule over the whole of society. In the Latin model, it was either an oligarchy in which one family or tight group of families ruled pretty much as feudal lords, or you had a president who was elected by a Congress who was elected by a tiny minority of economic elites. The U.S. model! In truth, Latin countries have not attempted true democracy until recent decades, maybe the last forty years. Given their relative impoverished states, this turn toward genuine democracy has occurred way too early in the national development process, and they are all paying the price for putting democracy first.

Democracy in Latin America is mainly undermined by the two-percent wealthy class who perpetually elects itself and then proceeds to put its own economic interests ahead of the nation's. In the cases such as Bolivia and Brazil, where indigenous labor leaders have come to power via popular elections, national development is undermined by seriously flawed policies, dependency on the welfare state and the leaders' movement toward more authoritarian style rule. In the case of Venezuela and others, they are hopelessly mired in the wrong kind of authoritarian rule and face very dim futures.

It so happens that Latin America is equally divided between Left-wing authoritarian regimes (all the wrong kind) and those with long, totally unstable democratic traditions. We need to examine why both remain poor and undeveloped, especially when viewed against the backdrop of the national development success stories in East Asia. The key factor is stability. Latin America is a wasteland of unstable growth and national development. The Asians have found that a cocktail of long-term stability, sound economic policies and a reasonable social compact is the key.

Many argue that it's a case of apples and oranges. The cultures of Latin American and East Asia are too different to be judged solely on the basis of conditions contributing to economic success. Nonsense. Ask our three-fingered alien friend KM. While culture does play a role, there is no substitute for sound economic planning and policies in national development. Those can be implemented regardless of cultural differences. And, since half of Latin America has an authoritarian tradition, why not adopt the model of Taiwan and Korea rather than the wrong kind? I don't buy the cultural difference argument. There are a few other more dominating factors that have left Latin America in the dust of their East Asian counterparts.

First among these is the adoption of the wrong kind of Social Compact, used both in the democracies and the authoritarian regimes in Latin America. Unlike the East Asians, the present-day Latins have used welfare states to placate the masses. Rather than have policies that are designed to deliver economic prosperity, they have sunk into the abyss of welfare states where oft times more than fifty percent of the national budget is dedicated to various forms of welfare. This helps keep the democracies and authoritarian regimes alike afloat. Presidents come and go, governments come and go, but in general, one thing never seems to change: Government buys the votes or allegiance of the masses by keeping the massive welfare state in place. This is a recipe for national development disaster, as clearly played out in Latin America. It keeps the underclass permanently down, whether intended or not. (shockingly, it seems there are cases in which it appears to be intended!). And, in recent years, popular elections (real democracy) have resulted in the underclass taking power (Bolivia, Ecuador…). This creates the polar opposite problem of the wealthy two-percent style rule. Both are bad, both lead nowhere in terms of economic progress.

The second reason contributing to the endless circle of poverty in Latin America is a shocking one. In nearly every Latin country, the society features a class of two-percent or so of extremely well off families who control nearly all aspects of national life, largely at the expense of the massive underclasses, or the 98 percent. Visitors to Latin America endure the endless scenes of the vast disparity between the haves and have nots. None of the Latin nations have achieved anything remotely resembling the egalitarian socio-economic success of the tigers in Asia. Indeed, they have gone entirely in the opposite direction. Invariably, the "common good" means to say what's best for the two-percent's circle of power, wealth and influence.

In most cases, it's a matter of pure class warfare. The wealthy seek to protect their economic interests and resist sharing the pie. They NEED the underclass to help perpetuate their lifestyles. It's a kind of servant class, that is also a borderline form of permanent indentured servitude.

In Panama, where I worked in 2010 on a nation brand project, I was repeatedly told by friends that the wealthy class protects its interests in even more heinous ways. The commonly heard charge is that the public education goes on neglected so that the underclass will not have the means to rise. It can be perpetually kept down by a totally worthless public education system, and by a system in which the poor have no means to enter private education. This is done, critics say, to preserve the lifestyle of the rich and powerful.

It's also a pattern that is seen throughout Latin America. Everything appears to be geared to preserve the wealth and power of the top two percent. It's no wonder a Hugo Chavez can rise to power in a place like Venezuela, or an Evo Morales in Bolivia. Even years after its discredit in the rest of the world, Communism or at least heavy – handed socialism, imposed by a strongman authoritarian rule of the worst type, still finds fertile ground in many countries of Latin America. That helps explain why countries are always teetering on the brink of falling into Chavez type rule. One might think that in the democratic countries of the region, if the masses have the right to vote, that they could at any time "change" the system. Not so. The upper class keeps them politically satisfied for the most part with welfare goodies. But it means keeping them down. It amounts to a trap.

Let's pause and take a snapshot of the history of democracy in a random selection of South and Central American countries. The clarity of the pattern that emerges is mind-boggling. It's almost as if one country can be used to represent the whole of the "democratic" experience in Latin America.

EL SALVADOR

Let's start small in Central America. El Salvador won its independence from Spain in 1821, close to the time most Latin countries achieved independence. It became a fully-functioning independent republic in 1838. The country started out with a Constitution, to be sure, but it was ruled by a series of oligarchies, akin to feudal lords. They traded turns at the public trough, a common condition on the Continent present all the way through to the present day. In the so-called Congress, wealthy land owners were granted super majority status, meaning they elected the Congress from among their own ranks (the U.S. model!). In El Salvador's case, one president after another (elected by Congress) changed the Constitution to suit his own interests and power-grabs.

El Salvador remained mired in constant peasant upheavals and turmoil well into the 20th Century. From 1931 to 1979, it experienced military dictatorship. Peasant revolts continued to be brutally suppressed. Nothing at all resembling sound economics was attempted, as the powerful interests fought to maintain their control.

In 1972, there was a brief window of opportunity when a reformist, Jose Napoleon Duarte, was elected. But corruption soon took over, and Duarte was ousted by a military junta. This is one of the patterns that happens over and over again in the Latin experience. A reformist leader emerges, gets popularly elected, and then is overthrown by a POPULARLY driven military coup a short time later. Sort of what happened to our pal Morsi in Egypt in 2013.

In 1979, a revolutionary Government Junta took

power. Civil war ensued. The U.S. supported the Government Junta, no matter how unpopular that was at home. Cuba and the Soviet-bloc supported the communist guerrillas and insurgents. By 1993, after more than a decade of destructive war like conditions at home, things began to stabilize as the insurgents were gradually defeated. Fortunately, the military junta chose to begin reducing its control and to open up. Elections occurred in 1994, '99, 2004 and '09, but now the country has gone to the other side of the Losers Circle, where zig zag national development is occurring at the hands of elites who take turns at the public trough. As a result, the nation is dirt poor. The current president, Mauricio Funes, appears to be a defender of the status quo, though there are increasing signs of some sound economic policies emerging, including talk about an alternative to the Panama Canal, and further development of the nation's main port.

In any case, El Salvador is but a poster child for the modern history of all of Latin America. Endless coups, juntas, authoritarian strongmen and self-interested oligarchies kept the nation embroiled in turmoil for its first 150 or so years. Today, its democracy that is holding the country down. It might be a better alternative to the constant upheaval of prior times, but the result is the same. The country stays mired in poverty and risks major instability at any time. It has not escaped the vicious circle of war, revolution and poverty. More is to come unless it comes up with a long-term national development plan that reins in democracy in exchange for a long period of prosperous growth. Its 2012 GDP per capita was $7,069, nearly one-fifth of the four tigers' average.

GUATEMALA

I could just keep this real simple and write "ditto for Guatemala." But it is very telling to lay out some more examples so that the patterns of Latin "democracy" reveal themselves for all to see.

This is a country with an ancient civilizational past, starting around 12,000B.C. The Mayan civilization arose around 2,000B.C. and lasted until 250 A.D. or so. It achieved incredible levels of both cultural and material development.

Modern Guatemala won its independence in 1840, after having been part of the First Mexican Empire (as were some of the other Central American states). In the Latin tradition, Guatemala has had periods of democracy (that early U.S. authoritarian model of oligarchs and such ruling) interspersed constantly with coups, revolutions, juntas and the like. It has been a stable democracy since 1996, but remains dirt poor for all the reasons repeatedly stated in this book. At best it is on a zig zag path to development; at worst, it is not on any path at all due to the constant changing of the guard and the two-percent stranglehold.

A look back at how Guatemala got here is, again, demonstrative of what ills Latin democracy. From 1931-44, the country endured the dictatorship of General Jorge Ubico. He was overthrown by a junta that then proceeded to rule over a relative calm, progressive period known as the Spring. In 1953, a form of land reform was even attempted, though the economic elites in the country quickly rose up to oppose it, mainly because it was coming from a leader, Jacobo Arbenz, who was openly aligned with Communists. The U.S. also supported actions against Arbenz, and he was soon ousted.

From 1960 to 1996 the country was devastated by a civil war that pitted rightists against leftists, the West against the Soviet-bloc. Vinicio Cerezo was elected in 1986, and quickly emerged as a reformer, but a series of failed coup attempts, social unrest, war weariness and a failing economy soon did him in. In 1996, urban elitist Alvaro Arzu won, but without much of any support from the agrarian sector, setting the country up for another round of peasant and labor unrest. Nevertheless, Arzu did start to put a dent in the nation's long running culture of corruption. He left a legacy of anti-corruption programs, but failed to move the dial on economic development, against the great odds of instability.

Guatemala has held two more presidential elections since, with Oscar Berger elected in 2003 (status quo) followed by Alvaro Colom's center-left win in 2007. Now, following a hundred and more years of poverty producing turmoil, it's full democracy that holds back the country. If it's not a case of oligarchical families taking their turns at the public trough, it's a case of zig zag development in which the next leader completely disavows the former's programs and heads in another direction altogether. Either way, the result is the same. The circle of poverty remains unbroken, and there is little light at the end of the tunnel. In 2012, its per capita GDP income was $3,300, one-tenth that of the four tigers.

NICARAGUA

Let's begin here in 1912-33. During this period, the country was run by a single family, the Chamorros, who were backed by the full power of the U.S. marines, who occupied the country. The U.S. used the barrel of a gun to extract economic favors for a shortlist of private U.S. companies. Massive bribes and other actions that would easily be considered illegal in today's context of international law were commonplace. This example of U.S. intervention was widespread in Central America, and in some cases throughout South America in the first half of the 20th Century. Thus, I would argue that the U.S. was once again complicit in the political ills of the continent and its failure to develop economically.

After 1926, the regime faced a series of civil conflicts which were brutally suppressed, with U.S. Aid.

In 1936, another family took power—the Samozas. They ruled with a tight fist until 1979, when a Sandanista-led communist rebellion overthrew him, despite his backing by the U.S. The Sandanistas had actually been around throughout the Seventies, embroiling the nation in a civil war in which atrocities were committed on both sides. After martial law was declared by Samoza in 1975, even more Government atrocities piled up, forcing the U.S. back into the uncomfortable position back home of having to support the devil it could live with versus the devil it couldn't—Soviet and Cuban backed Communist insurgents. But in the end, President Carter was forced to abandon Samoza and the let the chips fall where they may.

The Sandanistas, led by Daniel Ortega, and heavily supported by the Soviet-bloc and even North Korea, took power. The U.S., meanwhile, opted to continue supporting the anti-Communist group known as the Contras. Ortega was elected in 1984 to continue leading the country. But the election was not considered legitimate by international observers.

In 1990, something of a political miracle occurred when 1) the Communists decided to hold an open election for the presidency, and 2) they lost it to the National Opposition Union. It was actually a landslide by 14 points, even though many media reports at the time both in Nicaragua and the U.S. showed a Sandanista landslide in the making.

Things fell apart for the Union in the 1996 election when the winner, Arnuldo Aleman, was convicted of corruption. Special elections followed in 2001with Enrique Bolanos winning, followed by a startling comeback by a much more moderate Daniel Ortega in 2006.

But the story remains the same. The recent decade and a half of more stable democracy has done nothing for Nicaragua economically. The smallest of the Central American nations in terms of population, it should be better off by many accounts. It won't be so long as it remains married to the idea of democratic musical chairs. In 2012, its per capita GDP income was $1,757, one-twentieth that of the four tigers!

ARGENTINA

The South American continent is practically a political and economic mirror image of its Central American little brother.

We start with the saddest case of all, Argentina. One hundred and thirty years ago, even 100 years ago, Argentina was by far the richest country in Latin America and one of the top in the world. It is blessed with incredible natural resources and SHOULD still be one of the richest countries in the world. Instead, a course of national development ensued beginning in the 20th Century that has seen more periods of instability than stability. Today, Argentina is a basket case that always keeps observers on the edges of their seats, hoping that it will finally get its act together and get on the right path of development. Today, with its economy in shambles, there is little hope, and social unrest is starting to percolate again.

Argentina also gained its independence in the 1820s. But a long civil war ensued, lasting an incredible 37 years until 1862. That year, Bartolomew Mitre was made president, and he quickly began introducing a series of liberalizations. He opened the doors to expansive foreign investment, agrarian reforms, infrastructural constructions projects such as transportation networks and modernized ports. Much progress was being made, especially after some initial successes in rooting out remnants of feudal warlords.

Mitre's path is what should be known in Latin America as the right path. His rule was propped up by a technocracy and economic elites who shared his long-term visions for the rise of the nation. He was, shall we say, on the right path, with the right amount of powers and sound economic policies.

His National Autonomous Party crafted an unprecedented boom between 1880 and 1916, making Argentina one of the richest countries in the world. Increased European immigration, modernizations in the agricultural sector, huge levels of foreign investments, all contributed to the boom.

Then, wouldn't you know it—democracy got in the way. In 1916, with only ten percent of the 7.5 million Argentines voting, the left-wing Radical Civic Union (UCR) suddenly took power on the heels of labor unrest churned up by Socialist sympathizers. The new President, Hipolito Yregoyen, brought left-wing activism to the forefront of Argentine politics, forsaking the prior policies that had created decades of progress in the country. Labor movements became the fashion of the day, and mass instability ruled the country. This would begin Argentina's fall from grace, tearing the country apart and making economic progress almost impossible.

During what has later become known as the Infamous Decade, Yregoyen was overthrown by a military coup. This led to a long void of government control, and instability was the norm.

In 1946, the left-wing lunacy reared its ugly head again with the "election" of Juan Peron. For the next nine years he would embroil the country in labor strife, class warfare and general upheaval.

This was finally put to an end by a military coup in 1955. A series of see-sawing military interventions ensued until 1966, with an election interlude in 1963 in which neither Peronists nor Communists were allowed to participate. A coup in 1966 led by unions and students brought the "Revolucion Argentina" group to power. Contrary to their name, these new leaders sought to bring about socio-economic stability, and introduced a form of rule that later was coined as the"Authoritarian-Bureaucratic," or a four Asian Tiger like version of government, with soft authoritarian rule focusing on economics. Experts have called it neither democracy nor communism, and in fact, it did closely resemble what the Asian tigers were doing at the time.

Unfortunately, democracy would raise its ugly head again and turn back the clock. Dr. Hector Campura, an unapologetic Peronist, won election (including defeating a resurgent UCR) and he move unabashedly to re-instate Peronist style redistribution of wealth and protections for the domestic economy. Worse yet, Peron himself made a comeback in the election of 1973, winning more than 63% of the popular vote. The period of the welfare state was now taking root in a country that was not long before becoming rich off a free-market orientation. From here on out, the nation's bounty would be squandered by politicians seeking to make support for welfare programs from the underclass a permanent feature of Argentine politics.

In 1974, Isable Peron succeeded her husband in office. Soon, the bottom fell out as the bill for Peronist socialist policies came due. Rampant inflation strangled the economy and social unrest began to unfold once again. The Seventies and early Eighties were marked by constant social unrest, a stagnant economy as a result, and political impotence. Leftist and Rightists battled for the soul of the nation, with no clear winner emerging.

Then, in 1983, the nation returned to Constitutional rule with the election of Raul Alfonsin, a UCR candidate. Progress in national reconciliation ensued, with support for a vigorous democracy emerging again. But little progress was achieved on the economic front, and the pendulum of popular support on the heels of more social unrest once again swung back to the Peronists, who took power again in 1989.

The new president, Carlos Menem, was borderline authoritarian in his style of rule. He used excessive executive powers rather evenly, doing some good in overhauling the nation's economic infrastructure. It seemed he was putting Argentina back on the right track of soft-authoritarian rule focused on economic progress. But he could not break the shackles of the welfare state, and over burdened with that debt on society, his economy began to sputter. In 2001, the country entered another bad downturn, eventually hitting bottom, provoking the IMF and other world financial bodies to step in an attempt to rescue the Argentine economy. The next president, De La

Rua, committed political suicide by devaluing the currency, but only in the holdings of the middle class, not in the accounts held by wealthy Argentines. That insane move made him short-lived as president, and also spawned another round of national protests and unrest.

In 2002-03, the Peronist (now read Socialist) Eduardo Duhalda was elected president. His first step was to devalue the peso another 29%, bringing it down to one-fourth its former value. That launched the country into chaos, for Duhalda had not taken any appropriate steps to build a domestic consensus for this radical move. He was forced to hold new elections at the end of 2003, in which Nestor Kirchner took power. Kirchner, who was followed by his wife Cristina Fernandez de Kirchner into office, brought some long-sought stability to the nation. There has been some progress in recent years under Mrs. Kirchner, but Argentina is still subject to periods of domestic unrest as painful measures are taken to correct past bad policies.

Once among the world's richest nations, Argentina has been reduced to a basket case by decades and decades of unstable rule, whether by democratically elected leaders, military rulers or authoritarian strongmen. It does not matter. Argentina has yet to discover a viable path to sustainable development, and it is unlikely to do so so long as its democracy remains zero-sum in nature. Like other Latin nations, Argentina needs a strong leader or Party to set the right course for national development over a thirty-year period. Otherwise, its democratic tradition can be counted on to undermine any progress made in brief spurts. Personally, I still hold out great hopes for Argentina. It is blessed with tremendous natural resources and a diversity of capable people. It should be the powerhouse of Latin America. In 2012, Argentina's per capita GDP income was $11,576, one-third that of the four tigers, but certainly WAY under what it should be for a nation with such vast natural resources. It is important to keep in mind the contrast that the four tigers have absolutely NO natural resources, and relied on education, human talent, importing materials and spitting out exports to fuel their dramatic rises.

CHILE

Can you hear the record skipping yet?

Sharing a long border with Argentina, Chile also shares much of Argentina's unstable past. It, too, has been a battle ground for the West and Communism, the Left and the Right, and so on, and on.

In its first 150 years of the modern era, Chile was ruled by an elite group of families that vetted themselves for a turnstile approach to leadership. It was more feudal than anything. Between 1890 and 1925 it did experience what Chilean scholars call the Parliamentary Era, during which elites still ruled, trading places at the public trough, and basically spending most of their time quelling social unrest. That revolving door of elitist rule went on till the early Sixties when a Marxist-leaning dictator, Salvador Allende took power. Surrounded by KGB advisors and unabashedly aligned with the Soviet-bloc, Allende made

Chile the poster child for the Cold War's proxy wars. Chile became a battleground for the U.S. and Soviet Union, each using spurious espionage to undermine the other's interest in this resource rich country.

Allende, who had won an election with 35% of the vote, first introduced a typical form of Communist style land reform: Forcibly turn the land over to the peasants, without compensating the former landlords or owners. His efforts to nationalize important industries and increase public spending met with initial successes in bringing down unemployment and spurring economic activity. But this inflation-driven socialism, marked by wage increases, price controls and higher taxes, soon brought about a depression, starting in 1967 and lasting for six long years.

In 1973, the military and Chamber of Deputies (Parliament) had seen enough and overthrew Allende, replacing him with Supreme Commander Augusto Pinochet. Once again the democratic process had failed the nation. Pinochet ruled with a four-man junta, and moved quickly to suspend civil liberties, jailing thousands of oppositionists, and later committing numerous human rights atrocities that caught the world's attention. Again, the U.S. was caught up in the middle having supported Pinochet's ascent to power. It was once again forced to choose between the lesser of two devils, Pinochet versus Allende, in an oft-repeated story in the U.S.'s history of modern relationships with its neighbors to the south.

Pinochet erased much of the economic structure composed by Allende. He prohibited strikes and union activity altogether. He was able to make early progress but a severe recession kicked in, setting back efforts to win the people over with economic advances. Pinochet was elected to a further eight year term in 1980. During those years, Chile began to prosper as never before. Pinochet had surrounded himself not with KGB or CIA, but with technocrats from the University of Chicago, who later became known as the Chicago Boys. They helped steward the nation down a more stable path of economic growth. The group was led by Hernan Buchi, the Minister of Finance, who introduced more incentives and more sound planning. He got inflation under control and re-privatized many of the industries and companies that Allende had nationalized. Between 1984 and 90, Chile led all of South America with 5.9% GDP growth. Meanwhile, Chilean exports began to explode onto the scene, including such well-promoted items as wines.

In the process, the Government also began opening up with less controls on civil liberties, more freedom of speech and assembly.

But in 1990, Chileans went to the polls and rejected Pinochet's brand of authoritarian rule, deeming it still too harsh, despite the economic advances of the past ten years. 54.5% of Chileans cast their votes against him. Thus, another transition to democracy began, and is continuing to this day. The first years marked a period of national reconciliation, much like what Argentina went through. In 2006, the nation elected its first woman president, Michelle Bachelet, who had been left-leaning but took a decidedly quick turn to the center upon taking office. She was widely heralded around the world for her efforts to introduce sound economic policies. But, as with other Latin nations, her hands were tied by a national budget that focused more on maintenance of the welfare state. Her market oriented policies have clashed with that reality, and overall, she could probably have rated a solid B performance. She was succeeded in 2010 by Sebastien Pinera, who has assumed something of a status quo position.

Chile's political landscape was thrown a curve ball in 2000 when Pinochet returned home after having gone to London for surgery. While there, Spain had tried to extradite him so as to try him for crimes against humanity. But England did not budge, and instead let him return home to Chile. Upon his arrival, he was greeted by huge cheering crowds. Not all were former supporters. As the years passed by, many Chileans (probably not those who had family members "disappear" during his reign) became nostalgic about the economic good old days during Pinochet's rule. There was something of a national reconciliation underway, sort of a soul-searching on whether Pinochet was half-right or more about how to handle national development.

This writer would say he got it three-fourths right. There was just too much brutality and not enough successful social compact for my tastes. But I can understand why Chileans are beginning to reminisce about his period of rule. Under Pinochet, Chile had made more progress than in all of its previous years as a "republic" combined. In 2012, the per capita GDP of the country was a respectable $15,600, but still greatly underperforming when you look at the population versus the natural resources available for developing a stronger economy. Chileans simply are not using what they've got to improve their national lot. They need a plan. They need a strong leader. That GDP figure is just under half of the four tigers average, making Chile one of the more successful Latin American countries when it comes to economic development. How good could it be without changing directions every four years?

PERU

To Chile's north, another modern day leader in Peru got it nearly right. He is Alberto Fujimori, a gruff man of Japanese descent who became president in 1990.

But first, let's listen to that skipping record a bit.

In its early years of independence, through to about 1930, Peru was governed by aristocrats, meaning feudal lords using authoritarian means. They called it an "Aristocratic Republic," but that is just part of the overall Latin delusion with their democratic tradition.

Between 1930 and 1979, Peru alternated between corrupt democracies and military rule. Instability would be the correct adjective for describing the country, and it also explains why it remains mired in poverty even to this day. One case in particular stands out, that of Bustamante y Rivera, a president who tried to limit the power of the military and the oligarchs back in 1948, but who was quickly met with opposition from those very groups. He was overthrown.

Between 1968 and 1980, Peru only experienced military rule. It was not until 1985 that the country experienced its first peaceful transfer of power in the modern era. In 1990, things changed again with the election of Fujimori.

A mathematician by trade, Fujimori embarked on a clearly stated path of putting economics first. He took drastic measures to stabilize the economy and curb inflation (he lowered it a mere 7,000% !). He began introducing a series of economic incentives, and in 1992, took the extraordinary measure of disbanding Congress to hold new elections. Fujimori was moving carefully in the right direction of soft-authoritarian rule with a strong emphasis on the economy. His early tenure saw major economic reforms, a pro-investment climate take root and more privatization, all of which spurred unprecedented economic growth. He was the right man on the right track. I actually had the privilege of meeting him during a leadership conference in Singapore in 1995. He was at the height of his notoriety worldwide, but was certainly the darling of the East Asian nations. He was a short, stocky man with unusually massive hands, and after we shook hands I made a remark about them. He replied by saying, "One needs a good pair of these to change the course of a nation, while fighting a civil war." He was referring, of course, to his long battle against the Shining Path Maoist rebels in Peru. He had promised to eradicate the Communist rebel movement, and had already made much progress in doing so halfway through his tenure.

In 2000, Fujimori took steps to re-write the Constitution and allow himself a third term in office. But despite his success in bringing much economic progress to the country, Peruvians blinked. Social unrest broke out. People began to question his commitment to democracy and whether he was really seeking absolute power, as was the long held tradition on the continent. Fujimori fought to the end to defend himself as a selfless patriot dedicated to raising living standards via a focus on the economy. But he lost the argument, and was denied a third term. Not only that, but later on his opponents would seek to have him arrested for abuses of power. Fujimori fell out of the spotlight, but not before having successfully shown Peruvians a blueprint for economic success. His successor, Alejandro Toledo, continued much of the programs begun by Fujimori, including efforts to crush the resurgent Shining Path.

In 2006, Alan Garcia was elected president. Peru is doing okay economically, but it is still vulnerable to the kinds of unrest and revolts that have undermined its national development since Day One. In my view, Peruvians should have had the knowledge and courage to keep Fujimori on board for another ten years at least. That way a more solid foundation could have been laid for long-term national development. They missed a chance with the right guy at the right time. In 2012, Peru's GDP per capita income stood at $6,500, one-fifth of the four tigers' average. Again, woefully below what it should be.

BOLIVIA

Bolivia is an interesting case of what happens when the underclass takes over. The result is akin to what happened when Lenin took over Russia, or Mao in China. Economics go to pot.

Founded in 1825, Bolivia started out with a Constitutional Congress. But that window dressing did not last long. Soon, the nation was embroiled in an endless cycle of coups, oligarchical rule and other democracy misfires.

For twenty years, starting in 1964, the country was tightly ruled by a military junta. Elections in 1978, 79 and 80 were reported to be marked by widespread fraud. Each ended with no result.

With Congress electing the president, things changed in 1985 when Paz Estenssoro was chosen to lead the country. Pas presided over some relatively good years, marked by stability, and leading to a peaceful transfer of power in nationwide popular elections in 1989, with the election of Paz Zamora. The 1993 election was also deemed legitimate.

Landlocked, Bolivia is one of the poorest Latin countries. It has see sawed back and forth over the years between leftist and rightist governments. Pluralities in the country's elections have been as high as 32% and as low as 18%, a situation that breeds instability one election after another.

In 2002, for example, Sanche de Lozado was elected

president with 23% of the national vote. He lasted three years in office. In a 2005 election, Evo Morales, the first indigenous candidate for the nation's highest office, promised all kinds of socialist goodies to an impoverished electorate, and won easily with 54% of the vote. Morales went on to become a polarizing figure due to his lack of education, experience and general peasant behavior. The underclass supported him, and he took on more and more authoritarian style rule, introducing Communist style economic reforms and the like. Under his rule, Bolivia has gone nowhere, even though the Bolivian underclass may still consider him as their champion. In 2012, the per capita GDP income of the nation was stranded at $2,532, one-fifteenth that of the four tigers.

COLOMBIA: A Case Close to "Heart"

My work in Colombia from 2004-07 painted a bit of a different picture of the Latin condition. In Colombia, there is a larger percent of persons of Spanish descent than in most other Latin nations. Colombia also has larger racial and ethnic groups within its borders. Blacks to the Pacific side and Caribbean, Indians to the south and Hispanic "whites" in the center and in larger cities.

Under the administration of Alvaro Uribe between 2002 and 2010, Colombia emerged from behind the closed doors of its decades long civil war with Communist rebels and violent drug lords. Personal security was greatly enhanced, and a firm military hand backed by the U.S. pushed the FARC rebels way into remote jungle hideouts.

With the FARC decimated (though not entirely gone), Uribe could get on with the business of establishing the stable conditions needed for long-term economic development. He pushed a national consensus that put economics first, and at times resembled an authoritarian ruler if not simply a "sure of himself" paternalistic one. But because the nation was making such great progress on all fronts, Uribe was popular, and was even granted an extra-Constitutional second term as president.

When the nation was debating whether or not to allow an unprecedented second term for the president, I was asked by Mauricio Rodriguez, the editor of the nation's leading daily business journal (Portfolio), if I supported a second term for Uribe. I normally stay out of my nation clients' domestic affairs, but in this case, I chose to go with what I know, and told him that I did NOT support a second term for Uribe. Instead, I would support FOUR more terms for Uribe! Boy, no need to tell you how unpopular that idea was in a robust Latin democracy such as Colombia! Even Uribe supporters could not believe their ears and eyes!

In my view, Uribe would have been the best chance for Colombia to follow the national development model of the four tigers. Though he would have tremendous challenges in destructing the welfare state in Colombia, the implementation of a new Social Compact to offset that would have worked at that time, in my view. Uribe had displayed little inclination for typical Latin strongman rule. Rather, he took more of a paternalistic approach, not dissimilar to what Dr. Sun Yat-sen preached in his national development model for China. Uribe had the popularity, the know-how and the will power to build a consensus, a new social compact that would have a fighting chance at delivering a Stakeholder Society to Colombians. In my view, Uribe had the ingredients for success, including the lack of a penchant for abusing power.

Yes, there is always the human factor in which a Mugabe-type figure goes from being a potential savior to the most brutal dictator imaginable. But well into his first term, Uribe had shown an unrivaled commitment to bettering the lives of all Colombians, not just the ruling class. Of course, that would have been a tremendous challenge as well. Uribe also had on his side my client, Luis Guillermo Plata, one of the youngest economics ministers in the world, at age 39. Luis was highly decorated during his tenure as minister, with accolades mostly coming from abroad. He was rated by the World Trade Organization as the most effective minister one year, for his efforts to overhaul Colombia's trade regime toward more openness. What's important to note here is Luis' background. He spent some of his younger years growing up in Japan where his father served as a diplomat. He later served as Colombia's unofficial representative in Taipei, where I met him in 1995. He came to my office to express his admiration for our Made in Taiwan program, and said that it was his dream, both personally and professionally, to someday do something similar for Colombia's national image. He invited my partner, Jared Cameron, and I to visit the country in 1996. That was scary, quite frankly. The nation was still in lockdown practically. You could not go too far out from the cities. There were still bombings in the major cities. And, to make matters worse, the week we were there happened to be when then President Sampers had his U.S. visa revoked due to charges that he had been laundering drug money! In any case, my advice to Luis at that time was that it would be too early for Colombia to invest in a nation brand that had any hope for success. While I always preach that EVERY nation should promote itself (tourism, exports, investment), in Colombia's case the negatives still outweighed the positives. Later on, Luis became president of Proexport, Colombia's two-way trade promotion body, which also handles tourism and investment promotion. In between, he had gained a Harvard MBA and dabbled a bit in a Silicon Valley IT start up before joining Uribe's first election campaign. In 2002, after Uribe had been in office for a mere six months, Luis invited me to be a keynote speaker at a national leadership conference (Colombia Compite) held in Barranquilla. The other keynote speaker was Uribe. In the waiting room, I sat with the President and we discussed the key points of national development. He asked me what one thing I would do if I were in his shoes to lift the nation up economically. I told him I would implement a massive infrastructural plan centered upon building a nationwide network of interstate highways. Why? Because that is how you achieve egalitarian economic growth throughout all regions of the country, and secondly, it's a good way to create jobs and attract foreign aid money for the related construction projects. I sneaked in a second piece of advice as well: Get an image program going that would parallel his achievements in opening up the country and giving it the security environment needed for an economic boom to take hold!

We decided it was still a hair early for that, but in 2004, Luis invited me back to review progress. It was stunning. Colombia had changed unbelievably in a short two years under Uribe. Local economies were booming, visibly, all over the country. People were traveling within the country for the first time in decades. The time was clearly ripe for a nation brand project, and image campaign. All agreed and we moved forward, with Luis leading the way, and with Uribe correctly staying mostly out of the picture from then on out, for reasons stated earlier.

My point in relating these Colombia experiences revolves around Luis Plata and his background. Clearly inculcated with the success stories of the East Asian tigers, and clearly a Sinophile, Luis brought the kind of sound economic policies to bear on his own country, and to great benefit. During those years, Colombia boomed across the three most important factors of tourism, foreign investment attraction and exports. In fact, during Luis's reign as minister, all three sectors grew at rates over fifty percent a year, with foreign investment climbing in the hundreds of percentile growth. The credit should go to Uribe mostly because he had surrounded himself with a young crop of foreign educated technocrats (sound familiar!) who helped him change the face of Colombia. While the country is still massively burdened by dependency on the welfare state of old, there is still a boom going on as Colombia opens up to the world. Too bad, though. Another twenty years of Uribe and Colombia would do far more than just open up!

Contrast Uribe with what Hugo Chavez was doing in Venezuela at the time, and the picture is clearer. Chavez came to power as a result of the masses having been sold on what amounted to the promise of a massive welfare state, cloaked in the rosiest descriptions of socialism. He would spread the wealth and take care of the downtrodden masses. He certainly delivered. His Maoist brand of making everyone poor while ruling over the Animal Farm worked well and fanned popular discontent with capitalism and the West. Venezuela gradually took a place among the world's bad boy nations, being relegated to hanging out with the likes of Cuba, Russia, North Korea and Iran.

Meanwhile, Colombia began to boom. For the first time in decades the smaller towns and suburbs of the big cities were experiencing a wild rise in economic activity and growth. Exports soared, foreign investment skyrocketed and most astonishingly, given the nation's poor image for so long, tourism began to boom as well. Uribe led nothing short of a renaissance in Colombia, the re-birth of a nation, and one that has all the natural resources and human resources to potentially be what I often call the "Germany of South America."

Indeed, as part of my work in Colombia, I often interviewed other Latins about their views on Colombia. What I found was certainly enlightening. Most professed to be concerned about the potential rise of Colombia. They feared Colombia's economic potential, because it seemed to be on a course under Uribe that, unlike other Latin nations still mired in poverty-abetting systems, had great promise in delivering unprecedented prosperity to its people.

Another factor in Uribe's favor was his close ties to the U.S. Nearly alone among Latin nations in that regard, Uribe stuck by his guns, noting that historically it was better to align oneself with the U.S. or Western Europe rather than Russia or China, or with Left-wing authoritarianism, which had delivered nothing, and still fails to deliver anything, to Latin peoples. Uribe endured ridicule from other Latin leaders, and from the Left at home and abroad, but he knew better and stuck to his guns on this important national development issue.

At home, Uribe struggled with implementing policies that would lessen the welfare state burden, no matter how delicately so as to keep the masses in check. One day, after a Cabinet meeting (in which a couple ministers complained to him about the gringo in the room—said to be the first time anyone could remember a foreigner sitting in on an official Cabinet meeting, which was something par for the course for my work in developing nations), I had the privilege of traveling with the President, Luis Plata and the President's Chief of Staff on their version of Air Force One from Bogota to the city of Medellin, where Uribe was to attend the grand opening of a large new trade and exhibition center. On the flight, Uribe, who was sitting across the table from me, looked terribly flustered, and frankly, bent out of shape. He was upset about the day's media coverage on some of his more painful domestic policies. I finally broke the silence by telling him, "Look, man, so what if you are having a bad day. You are having a history making four years. Hang in there!." He didn't say anything, but seemed to appreciate this bit of good cheer. Later, upon arriving at Medellin's airport located high up on the rim of the bowl that the city itself sits in, we transferred to Blackhawk helicopters, with the four of us in one, and a back up one for escort. We flew down into Medellin through incredibly densely forested gorges. A big thrill for me, but I could tell Uribe would not agree. Here was the man, who had exhibited every day the tremendous courage needed to change a nation, revealing an awkwardly strange fear of flying! After landing off a downtown street, our motorcade made its way through the back streets of Medellin, where Uribe hails from. The thrill grew as I experienced first hand his tremendous popularity. Crowds lined the streets, and as we got out of the cars at the Exhibition Center, I could hear some in the crowd wondering who the gringo was. I keep my hair short, so I probably looked the part of a U.S. Special Forces guy out of uniform. It was a great ride…

Later on during my work on the nation brand, I was asked by Portfolio what policies I thought were key to nation-building. I boldly offered my observation that Colombia, not to mention just about every Latin nation, is ripe for the kind of Land Reform that Taiwan implemented in 1950. What I had observed in Colombia was certainly unsettling. The wealthy class owns nearly all the land outside the cities, and using Bogota as an example, they have their vacation villas sprinkled all over the lush countryside and hillsides. The problem with this is that it is a colossal waste of national economic resources. Instead of being used simply as the "view" for the wealthy, this land should be tilled, creating millions of jobs and a clear base for exceptional agrarian-based economic progress. It turns out that Colombia is unique with its year round growing seasons. It can and should be one of the world's top producers of foodstuffs. It can develop huge light industries processing foods for domestic and export markets.

What's needed is land reform. A Taiwan style program that turns the land over to those who would till it. In such a system, the tillers are incentivized to produce wildly. The former land owners, in turn, can be compensated with shares in State owned businesses, or in the industries that spring up as a result of the new agrarian production. We'll cover this subject more thoroughly in our section on Taiwan. But, it probably goes without saying that the idea did not go over very well among Colombia's ruling class. Can't give up that wonderful view, for anything! I will mention, however, that one of my closest Colombian friends, Jose Perez, who made his initial fortunes in textiles, has actually implemented personal land reform on his farms outside Bogota. Instead of sitting on a villa overlooking a lush valley, Jose turned hundreds of acres into a series of rose farms. He personally increased employment in the nearby area by many times. He's an economic hero. More need to follow his example.

The other countries in Latin America that are thought to have much potential are Brazil and Argentina. Unfortunately for both, neither is on a sensible path of national development. They are either bogged down by Left-supported welfare states, or by democracies that fail to deliver on economics, year in and year out, and president after president.

First Argentina. What a basket case. We already noted that between 1880 and 1916, Argentina was one of the richest countries in the world In fact, around fourth or fifth richest (thinking The Philippines, anyone?!). Until Marxism, socialism and the politics of the Left were allowed to take root, take over and lure the masses into the trap of a perpetual state of poverty and instability.

When I think of potential, I think of Argentina with its vast natural resources and tremendous human capital. It has nearly all the ingredients for success except one: It has no plan for success. It would rather stay mired in unstable democratic politics rather than get down to serious brass tacks about how to make the obvious happen. What a huge price Argentina pays for its love of democracy and the bankrupting economic policies that result from the perpetual need to win votes by keeping the welfare state in place. One gargantuan pity.

Brazil, on the other hand, has begun to achieve some success as a rising economic power. It is proudly a BRIC nation, along with China, Russia and India, placing it among the top four of rapidly emerging economic powers. A fifth rising power South Africa, was later admitted to the club, which now goes by the acronym BRICS.

But Brazil's rise may not last long, however. With a Socialist president and a country where the poverty rate is way over fifty percent, there is no future for the Brazilian economy on its current path. The weight of the welfare regime will collapse upon itself. The wealthy classes will continue to resist change, and the nation that already has the highest rates of crime will get even worse in that category. Unless Brazil comes up with a social compact that makes sense, and unless that is followed by a sensible economic development plan implemented by a soft, enlightened authoritarian ruling body, Brazil will not make it much further down the path of development. It is essentially winging it right now, playing on small victories like the Olympics and World Cup to placate the disgruntled masses at home. That won't work for long, and Brazil will be left perpetually poor, unable to escape the vicious circle of poverty, instability and violence that causes most of the continent to trail East Asia in development. As I write this into the summer of 2013, violent labor and other protests continue to rock Brazil's largest cities. The country needs something grander than an Olympics, and something other than a welfare state delivered by its democracy. Colombia's GDP per capita income reached $7,855, and is on the rise. Overall, Colombia has experienced the highest growth rates in Lat Am in recent years. Now that the country's years of isolation are coming to an end, expect to see Colombia emerge as the growth leader for years to come. That is, if its democracy does not get in the way!

PANAMA: The Little, Big Under-Achiever

In 2010 I had the privilege of having been asked to assist Panama with a nation-branding exercise. I was invited by the advertising agency BBM, who was working with Panama's Tourism department to craft a new umbrella brand image for the country. It was my first visit to Panama.

My wife Chenya and I immediately fell in love with the place. Panama has it all. Fabulous city life in Panama City, beach life within a few miles in either direction east or west (to Atlantic and Pacific oceans) and incredible jungle environs right outside the main city and beyond. It has mountain climates along side tropical.

Panama is also exciting because of its diversity of people and endless energy when it comes to artistic and creative endeavors. If Panamanians are anything, they are resourceful.

With all these blessings, however, no visitor to Panama leaves without being disappointed about the mass poverty across the tiny, isthmus nation. And it's the kind of poverty that makes one shake your head, wondering how it could happen given the country's history of close ties to the U.S. and its abundance of natural resources.

Panama is actually a poster child of the worst kind for what's wrong with many Latin democracies. The two-percent rules, and elections are merely a cover for a musical chairs process that brings one family to the public trough after the other. The goal seems to be to gain as much power and economic advantage as possible for oneself and cronies before moving on down the line.

Panama is also likely guilty of the worst kind of democracy in that the two percent protects its interests by giving the underclasses very little opportunity to rise. For example, many Panamanians point out that the reason the public education system is nearly useless is because the wealthy use the decrepit system to keep the underclasses down, so that they will perpetually feed the servant class upon which the wealthy have come to depend for their own good life. This is a startling accusation, but when you look at the state of public schools in the country (many don't have desks, supplies, etc.), you can't help but think there is much credence to what the critics are saying.

We have discussed all along here the role of the two-percent in suppressing real democracy. In this case, Panama serves as an example of how they also suppress the economy to protect their way of life, power and so on. The problem is exacerbated when the elites compete fiercely among themselves, putting the national interest way back in the priority line, behind their own selfish interests. Panama needs a strong leader who will transcend this narcissism of the elite, and put the country first. It can be rich. Real rich.

There are other reasons why Panama continues to wallow in poverty. Chief among these is the constant fighting that goes on between the oligarchs. While they do certain things to protect their interests as a whole, not a day goes by where they are not fighting among themselves, or competing for money, power and influence. It gets ugly. I already related the story of how my interview process was made interesting by the powers-that-be criticizing the other powers-that-be, at almost every interview. They basically hate each other. And their elite competition is not just annoying, it actually severely harms the national interest.

Let's put it real simply. Panama SHOULD be rich. Its history certainly suggests so. The country was formed for one reason: The U.S. wanted to build a canal, but ended up having to buy the isthmus from a Colombian first (Panama was originally part of Colombia until this purchase). With the land in hand, the U.S. then proceeded to build the canal.

Panama began as a republic in name only as it was totally dominated by families who controlled the economy. In 1909 it was granted separation from Colombia, but did not formally become independent until 1921.

But her independence was relative in the sense that the U.S continued to occupy the entire Canal Zone as a formal U.S. territory. It was not until 1977 that President Jimmy Carter signed a treaty that would see the turn over of the Canal to Panamanian sovereignty on January 1, 1990.

Panama, however, was in for a rocky political ride in the lead up to the transfer. Since the Fifties, the military was carving out an increasingly larger role for itself in the nation's governance. One military leader, General Omar Torrijos, actually enjoyed much popularity at home for introducing welfare measures and the like to appeal to the poor majority. Torrijos, however, died in an unexplained plane crash in 1981. He was succeeded by Manuel Noriega, who later became one of the best known members of the Latin American Authoritarian Leaders Hall of Shame.

Noriega constantly locked horns with U.S. President Reagan throughout the Eighties. In short, he lost, as the U.S. invaded Panama in December 1989. Noriega was captured and extradited to the U.S.

In hindsight, Panamanians are ambivalent about the U.S. invasion. Many see it as having saved the nation from a brutal dictator, while others, agreeing with that assessment, still feel hurt by the intervention of a foreign power.

Since Noriega, Panama has maintained a stable political environment marked by a series of valid elections (as opposed to Noriega, for instance, who voided elections if he lost them—1989).

However, Panama's democracy has not served the nation's interest in any meaningful way. The oligarchs are still around, and their grip on power is uncontested . None of the presidents has shown any inclination to tackle poverty, instead relying on welfare mechanisms to placate voters. This is a terrible burden on the small nation's budget.

One of the really fascinating things about Panama is the way the poor embrace their natural environment. During my research for the brand identity, I did not limit my target audience to influencers; I also interviewed folks on the streets, in some cases, dirt poor, unemployed youth just hanging out. One day, we interviewed a group of three such guys. Around 20 years of age, they had no jobs and confessed that they did not really need jobs to get by. The jungle, just minutes away, could provide fruits for nutrition for free; the ocean, just a block away, could provide nourishment. So, these guys were not about to starve. They had mastered the trick of relying on Panama's rich natural blessings. Hmmm.

Despite all these anomalies, I still feel Panama has truly great potential. One of history's great ironies is that the Panamanians have done a much better job of managing the Canal than we Americans did. For a simple reason: The Panamanians manage it as a business, whereas the U.S. managed it mainly as a military zone. And, as most of us would agree, the private sector would manage this type of business much more efficiently and effectively than a government would.

Panama is all about connectivity. Its very founding was based on the need for the Canal. It cannot escape its destiny as a connector of lands, oceans, peoples and eco-spheres. Panama is uniquely blessed to play a connectivity role in world commerce, and indeed, its GNP is still nearly 80% dependent on the Canal and its related business activities, including shipping, banking, insurance, trade and so on. Given its small size, natural bounty and location, location, location, Panama SHOULD be destined for tremendous prosperity. What holds it back is a bad form of democracy that has taken root long before a Stakeholder Society developed. With all it has going for it, Panama could eventually pan out a little better like Costa Rica. But that will require the two-percent to relinquish some space at the trough for the masses. It is a terrible shame that a handful of families get to enjoy the benefits of this naturally blessed nation. Panama is a success story waiting to happen, when the right leader, and the right plan finally comes along.

COSTA RICA: A Potential Fly in Dave's Ointment

In the interest of full disclosure, open-mindedness and candor…Costa Rica is the ONE country in the world that partially debunks my assertions about the harm done by putting democracy first.

This little dynamo in Central America, sandwiched between Panama to the south and Nicaragua to the north, is one of the best performing nations in the world over the past thirty or so years. It has enjoyed a robust democracy since 1953, and unlike its Latin cousins, really only had one or two periods of major political upheaval to scar its past. It experienced a short-lived dictatorship in 1917-19, but the worst was in 1948 when a civil war broke out over President Rafael Calderon's refusal to step down after he lost an election. An exiled leader, Jose Maria Figueres Ferrer, returned home to defeat the forces loyal to Calderon. Figureres then took over the reins and brought about welcome changes in the socio-economic-political affairs of the nation. He severely limited the role of the military in political affairs. As a result Figureres became a national hero, leaving behind a lasting legacy of liberal reforms, which also set the stage for stable democracy to emerge. The country has had 13 good elections since 1953. One president in particular stood out as a champion of focusing on the economy, and that was Oscar Arias Sanchez, whose close ties to Taiwan gave him much knowledge and a deep understanding about economic development.

Unfortunately, however, I can argue that Costa Rica

only debunks half my assertion about the harm of democracy. The country's per capita GDP is still a measly $9,670, above average for the continent, but still way below that of the four tigers. That should not be. What's holding back Costa Rica at all is its zig zag approach to national development. Every four years, with every new president, the country changes its course just enough to set it back. You can tell this by economic growth figures, which show a marked zig zag climb, nothing like the thirty straight years of upward slant achieved by the Asian tigers, and now China.

Like Colombia, in the case of Uribe, Costa Rica had a chance to stay the course with Oscar Arias. He was the right guy at the right time. Another twenty years of his policies and Costa Rica would be at $25,000 per capita GDP income levels! But since Costa Ricans have already been programmed to put democracy first, it is likely they will just have to stay on the slow boat to prosperity. That is a risky thing, given the growing disparity between haves and have-nots in the country, and throughout the continent. But, it may be just the way it is.

Latin America in Review

It should be crystal clear why this continent has failed. It should also be clear as to why I presented this brief walk-through of the continent's so-called democratic traditions (or lack thereof, of course).

These countries have been under military or bad

authoritarian rule for much of their modern eras. They
have experienced a constant see-saw of leftist-rightist
policies. They have been hurt by Cold War and other Great
Power rivalries. They have been hurt often by misguided
or inappropriate U.S. policies, not to mention a severe lack
of intelligent guidance from the U.S. Nearly all of them
have developed political cultures that are anything but
conducive to economic development. They have been and
continue to be, on average, governed by oligarchies, or
families who put their own interests above the national
interest, or suppress the underclass to protect their own
interests.

They are dirt poor contrasted with their East Asian
counterparts. And it's mainly all because they continue to
put a rotten democratic tradition ahead of the more
important nation-building issue of economic development.
In other words, so long as they continue to put democracy
first, and not economics, they will not likely reach a
Stakeholder Society stage of development that is required
for real, stable democracy to take root. They will not
escape the vicious circle of instability that breeds poverty
rates that outstrip GDP growth rates.

And speaking of growth rates, it is important to note
here that Latin America needs to do the kindergarten math.
When you have 50% or more of your population below the
poverty line, and your poverty growth rate is 7%, and your
GNP growth is a constantly anemic 1 to 3%, guess what?
You're going to be perpetually impoverished. Every Latin
American nation needs to come up with a formula, both
politically and economically (and that is socially bearable),

that will create the conditions for 8-12% growth over a 25-year period, straight. That is the only way to defeat poverty. The four tigers proved this. If you don't get the politics right, you will continue to risk having zig zag growth, which can lead to destabilization of the society and thus inhibit economic growth. This is always more of an unstable state than not because it is next to impossible for a leader to implement good change in the confines of a three or four year term, only to have the next guy come along and negate it. This pattern repeats itself in Latin America. It explains why Argentina, for example, kept swinging back from Peronists to the UCR and back again every four years or so. The leader did not have time to succeed, and before he could, the discontent of the folks was too high, and social upheaval led to another change in power. This is one of the key reasons why democracy is clearly not suitable in the early stages of economic development. It takes time for sound economic policies to take hold and begin to make a difference in people's lives. But it need not take centuries, as the Four Tigers demonstrated. Patience is a tough thing to own when you own little else, and Latin America always seem to remain at risk for social strife, upheaval and even civil war between the haves and have-nots. Welfare states are but a band-aid on the problem. The deeper wounds and scars do not respond well to band-aid treatments. Poverty sucks for anyone, and so long as the folks have no hope at best and no social compact that makes sense for them to have patience at the least, then nations are at risk of perpetuating poverty.

The challenge is doubled if the elites who own power don't get along and put their competing interests above the national interest. At least the Founding Fathers in the USA had enough shared interests (mostly economic, since they fought often over politics and matters of governance) to keep the boat mainly afloat until the Stakeholder Society point was reached (notwithstanding that little matter of a Civil War, fought over economic priorities and ways of life!).

Today, after having been stung repeatedly by the wasp of strongman rule, many Latin American nations have embellished their democracies with what most consider to be a good feature: Term limits. Not a good idea at all. I get the psychology behind it, after two hundred years of bad authoritarian rule. But, the truth is that term limits lead to the second scourge of democracy—the zig zag path of development. Term limits will almost guarantee failure in terms of achieving the economic growth rates needed to pull these nations out of poverty. But the West won't help matters. It is a commonly held belief there, too, that term limits are a good thing. Maybe in developed economies, but certainly not in impoverished nation-states. It's time for an era of intelligent social compacts.

Only some countries were highlighted here. Nearly all the others fit the same pattern. This would include some of the poorest of the poor, such as Honduras, Paraguay and Ecuador to name a few more. One country that deserves mention for its recent opening up and attempts to make the "right" moves is Uruguay. With its coastline, natural resources and resourceful people, Uruguay is starting to make waves in positive ways on the Continent. Its per capita GDP has risen well lately, and is up to near Chile's level at $15,000. Good on you, Uruguay.

I used Latin America to make the case for my argument that both bad authoritarian rule and the wrong kind of democracy can hold nations back from achieving prosperity and successful national development. Africa, which is much worse than Latin America in this regard, probably needs mention, too…

AFRICA: The Lost Continent

Since Africa is a lot worse off than Latin America, there is no need to dwell on it much in these pages. I think Latin America adequately proves the point about the wrong kind of authoritarian rule and democracy both being bad for national development. Why pile on with the African experience?

I do, however, find certain statistics about Africa helpful. Never mind that this is where human civilization got its start. Getting out of the blocks first has certainly proven to be no advantage. On the whole, Africa is clearly the most backward place in the world, save for a handful of ancient jungle tribes still around, and oh yes, that star of Communism, North Korea.

I would simply recommend that folks read the book 'The Shattered Continent," by former ECONOMIST reporter James Hicks. It lays out the case for why Africa has failed probably better and in an easier to read fashion than any other work I know of.

Back to those insightful facts. A glance at the World Bank's list of per capita GDP incomes by country says it all. Of 190 nations and territories listed, South Africa comes in at the highest rank at 73. Not bad, really, but many dismiss it as being somewhat apart from the overall African experience given its history of European settlement and governance. There's a story to be told there, and Hicks does it well.

It's the rest of sub-Sahara Africa that is truly frightful. African nations make up nearly the entire bottom eighth of the GDP per capita income list. Nearly all of them are under $1,000 per annum incomes. The exceptions you can count on one hand: South Africa, Angola, Namibia, Ghana and Nigeria, with the last two just above $1,000. These are Stone Age numbers contrasted with what the East Asians have been putting up in recent decades.

Granted, Africa presents a more complicated set of circumstances, namely derived from cultural influences. Both nomadic tribes and those wedded to the idea of staying put in their tribal lands are doomed to poverty. There's not much point to living in a desert unless, of course, your "culture" requires it. Culture ends up binding tens of millions of Africans to areas that are generally considered uninhabitable. Yet, Western aid is supposed to carry them past that small consideration, perhaps in perpetuity. Culture is the toughest thing to change when it comes to national development. So it's easy to see how you can spin your wheels in terms of trying to come up with solutions to Africa's horrific poverty and disease. At times, I just want to tell them to move to where the food is, but most of them won't even do that. No can do culturally.

On top of the culture dilemma or straight-jacket, you have the business of brutal strongman rule. The wrong kind of authoritarian rule again. The post-colonial history of independent states in Africa is replete with that same old broken record of one mass murder following another, one pillager of the nation's resources following another, and so on. The rule in Africa is that brutal rule is the rule, and foreign observers always seem to be left thinking that the Continent as a whole has little or no regard for human life, let alone what might be mistaken for a national interest committed to bettering peoples' lives.

Where do you even start? We have already covered the likes of Mugabe in the section on Strongmen Gone Wild. Rwanda made headlines with near genocidal massacres, as has The Sudan. Uganda had one of the all – time greats in Idi Amin. Indeed, massacres and other forms of brutal shakedowns of one's opponents seems to be the norm, not the exception, on the Continent even today. This goes for the supposed democracies as well. More often than not they have experienced coups, juntas and strongmen who won't step down after losing elections.

The deaths of millions and millions of innocents at the hands of brutal dictators and their usually out of control military comrades is bad enough when examining the development of this Continent. But there are other bad things such as the unfathomable squandering of natural resources that occurs. One leader after another takes his turn at pillaging the trough of valuable resources, putting

95 cents out of every dollar in his own pocket. For a resource-rich Continent, is this not a colossal shame? Shouldn't the nation-states of Africa be taking advantage of their resources to nurture prosperity for all? Not going to happen so long as democracy is a joke and the culture of the wrong kind of strongman rule continues to strangle them.

Great leaders have arose recently in Africa, but unfortunately, their impacts were mainly in the political arena. Bishop Desmond Tutu and Nelson Mandela are the stars in this category, of course. They righted past wrongs in the important area of human rights, but have had little influence on economics. Can't blame either of them for they are not economists nor did they have any essential background in national development.

What's needed is a good, long dose of the right kind of authoritarian rule. Social compacts that set out the costs-benefits of such rule, so long as the compact is acted upon by both the strongman ruler and the public who is asked to sacrifice certain civil liberties along the way.

Some African nations have fairly decent democracies, including Kenya and Ghana. But then that is part of the problem. Look at their respective per capita GDPs: $977 and $1,562. They are at the middle of the pack in Africa. That would mean democracy has not served them very well at all. Cronyism, rampant corruption and other "cultural" diseases contribute most to the perpetual state of poverty. It's a really sad thing when experts contend that often times 95 cents out of every dollar allocated for a national development project disappears into the pockets of the inner-ruling circle. That simply adds up to hopelessness. Unless the right kind of leader finally emerges, and is given the necessary time, bought with a proper social compact, to lead the nation out of poverty.

In recent years, Africa has been slightly improving. Some are calling it the next big wave in world development. Nations are waking up to the potential of their resources, and are taking fuller control of them versus the foreign multinational corporations. More and more leaders are committing themselves to national infrastructural projects such as roads, ports, railways, airports, power plants and so on. Corruption remains a major drag on all of it, but the picture is improving.

The real flies in the ointment are the cultural shackles, bad types of authoritarian rule (Zimbabwe) and terribly flawed democracy. One can only have high hopes for Africa, but it has so much to overcome, even to put a mere dent in the poverty levels. Africa certainly would be better off if it Just Says No to Democracy, and to bad authoritarian rule. Once a great leader emerges who puts the national interest first, the nation should embrace that leader for as long as they can, and for so long as he or she continues to produce results.

There are a million reasons why that sounds pie-in-the-sky or easier said than done. On the other hand, as we have argued here, there are models of development, experiences from elsewhere, to learn from. That kind of change is reasonable, and it only takes a great leader to get in and make history.

It's time to move on to how national development should be done. We are going to use Taiwan as the best experience for how the economics first model creates the best conditions for democratic development.

But first, it is instructive to take a cursory look at the philosophical underpinnings of the blueprint Taiwan used to achieve its amazing economic progress and the robust democracy that followed. The teachings of two historical figures in China, one the ancient sage Confucius, and the other the founder of republicanism in modern China, Dr. Sun Yat-sen, are critical to our understanding of why democracy is developing the way it is in the context of the modern Chinese state. The influence of Confucius helps us understand why authoritarian rule is more the rule rather than the exception in China's long history, and Dr. Sun's teachings are instrumental in providing a blueprint on how to bridge that deeply rooted authoritarian tradition with the movement toward democracy.

6 THE TEACHINGS OF CONFUCIUS AND DR. SUN

In any discussion of the development of Chinese culture and civilization, it is impossible to leave out the influence that the teachings of the ancient sage Confucius have had on the world's oldest continuous living society. Confucius' thought is the pillar upon which this great culture has built its enduring institutions and ways of thinking and indeed, its way of life. Confucius' teachings on social structure, morality and behavior permeate nearly every aspect of life in China, still after 2,500 years.

History grants Confucius his earned spot in the pantheon of the most influential persons who ever lived, there among Jesus of Nazareth, Buddha and Mohammed. But unlike the others, Confucius is not a religious figure, but rather a sage who laid out social and political norms based on a series of interlocking relationships in life that form the "glue" that holds civilized society together. Confucianism is more a way of life, a framework for how individuals should behave within the interlocking relationships that form the basic building blocks of society. These relationships included father-son, mother-son, teacher-student, elder-youth, master-servant, emperor-subject and government official-citizen. If followed, the hierarchical behavioral standards set forth by Confucius lead to the attainment of peace and harmony in society, not just in China but the world as well. This Confucius called the "da tong," or "Great Doctrine," a social contract that seeks to create universal harmony, and he made its attainment the goal of any individual, any government, any nation.

Achievement of the "da tong" proved quite challenging throughout China's history. Indeed, it we look back over 3,000 years, you see a China that experienced division more often than unity as a single nation-state. Provincialism and tribalism were the main culprits, with competing interests constantly vying for dominance, even within the context of a homogeneous culture.

Interestingly, over the millennia, those Chinese dynasties that adhered to Confucianism tended to last longer than those that tried to repudiate and eradicate the influence of Confucius. This fact is obviously not lost on today's Chinese Communist Party. Seeing that historical trend, the Party decided to rehabilitate Confucius after three decades of condemning his teachings as a core part of the Old China, which Mao had overthrown and replaced with a violent form of Marxist thought. The "return" of Confucius to high stature in China is best revealed by the statue of the sage now adorning Tiananmen Square in Beijing, where upon Confucius showed up in 2008. Previously, only Mao held that highest accolade of a presence on this sacred ground in the nation's capital.

It is important to note here that China's enduring culture is not an accident of man or nature, but rather the result of its incredibly strong roots, mostly in Confucianism. Over the millennia, China has been invaded by foreigners, including the Mongolians (1276), the Manchus (1611) and so on. But each time, the foreigners ended up being assimilated into Han Chinese culture. The culture proved too strong to be replaced or affected by foreign influences. Anything imported eventually turns Chinese, proving the ultimate strength of the world's greatest culture. This includes religions, such as Buddhism, which now has a distinct Chinese version from that of the original Indian one.

Fast-forward to the present day. Marxism and its Soviet manifestations were imported into China. They are now fading fast. No communism exists in China, and the Communist Party today merely pays lip service to its Marxist roots. The truth is that this foreign ideology is already well on the way to being entirely undone by Chinese culture. As we said before, one clear sign that the Party is aware of this influence is their programmed rehabilitation of Confucius. The great sage is making a stunning comeback after decades of suppression. That suppression reached its pinnacle, perhaps, during Mao's maniacal Cultural Revolution, 1966-76. That was the period in which Mao sought to completely rid China of all vestiges of traditional culture, with an eye toward replacing it with a new man, a new "ism." The Confucius home and temple in Qufu, Shandong Province, were particularly vulnerable to the machinations of the young Red Guards whom Mao had unleashed to carry out the final decimation of traditional culture. Red Guards, led by a young woman from Beijing, showed up and tried to burn down the temple and destroy the stone monuments brought to the temple over two millennia by emperors paying homage to the sage. But the Qufu villagers fought back in a rare show of defiance, and the damage was limited. Despite the incredible violence used to bury the past, the effort, like all those before it, failed. Other attacks came from the outside; this one from within, but even so, it failed to overcome the millennia old power of Chinese culture. And thus we have a score card: Confucius 1, Mao 0. Indeed, the card should just say: Confucius 1, Anyone Else 0. Ever.

Thus it is that any political movement or even total revolution runs the risk of self-defeat if it does not include the proper dose of Confucius thought and tries to deviate too much from the Confucian "glue" that forms the foundation of a culture that is here to stay.

But Confucius is not infallible. His teachings left one major hole in society that has much bearing on the issue of democracy's ability to take root in a traditional Chinese society. In reality, Confucius was a fan of dictatorial, or at best authoritarian, imperial rule. His relationships begin with the emperor, and in a purely hierarchical fashion, work their way down from the top through all levels of society. We already mentioned how this is achieved by multiple layers of paired relationships that together form the building blocks of civil society. But there is no mistaking that a major reason Chinese today are so amenable to authoritarian rule is because they have been ingrained with such thought all along, both at home and in the schools. Rare is the free-spirited Chinese who ventures outside the norm of the accepted authoritarian, hierarchical structure of society inculcated in Chinese by the deep roots of Confucian thought. Given the power of the culture, one can go as far to say that democracy is an unnatural concept to most Chinese.

Confucian thought has created one other peculiar dilemma for modern China as he left out one critical relationship that MODERN society cannot do without: That of the citizen to citizen relationship. In Confucius day, the emperor was the ultimate authority, while the family or clan was the next critical building block of society. In his series of paired relationships, he never referred to the individual citizen's role or responsibility, having assumed that if everyone followed the behavioral norms of his relationship structure, society would run fine. To be fair, however, in Confucius day, there really was no such thing as a "citizen." Society was feudal, and the common men were all equal in the context of their serfdom. Confucius' paired, hierarchical relationships all involved one person being subjugated by the other or one having to show respect to the other, with one paired relationship built on top of the next, creating a foundation for social stability. There was, in his times, no reason to consider a citizen to citizen relationship because they were equals. Or, it can also be argued that citizens all fell under the "master-servant" unit in the full hierarchy.

Despite that shortcoming in his teachings, Confucius did dwell much on the subject of the "common good" or "da tong" as it is known in Chinese. Confucius definitely believed that all men should be conformists as a means of holding society together. Thus precepts and practices tied to the concept of the common good are common themes deeply imbedded in Chinese culture. Chinese are raised to be good team players, and individualism is frowned upon, even in today's more wild west capitalist system. They are taught to sacrifice for the common good. This and the other aspects of Confucius thought discussed above help explain why Chinese in general are not opposed to authoritarian rule, and why, down the road, the development of democracy may be a hard road to hoe.

Today, however, the lack of any notion of the citizen to citizen relationship has led to a situation in which Chinese society appears largely uncivil on the surface. When this writer first visited Taiwan in 1978, the island was still adversely affected by the lack of civility that can only be achieved if there is some sort of well-ingrained understanding of the norms of behavior on how citizens should treat each other in the context of modern society. The symptoms of this "hole" in Confucian thought are well known to foreigners who lived in Taiwan back then and who live in Mainland China today. It's a dog eat dog world out in public. Every man for himself. People don't follow basic accepted norms such as standing in line to board buses and trains. They treat unfamiliar fellow citizens like crap, right out in public. Traffic rules don't matter, and when hundreds of millions of narcissists are involved, the result is pure chaos. Chinese call it "organized disorder," but what it really is is a lack of public civility. The culprit here is Confucius himself since he did not teach Chinese how to treat each other outside of the relationships cited above. The Chinese call it "gong de xin," or "public virtue heart." And foreign visitors to China today see in plain view out on the streets how this loophole or shortcoming in Confucian thought adversely effects modern Chinese society.

But there is hope. In Taiwan today, one sees a very civil society. It was gained over about four decades of education and—wouldn't you know it—the power of the pocketbook. Chinese also care deeply about economics, and regulating their behavior through heavy fines gradually brings them around to understanding the importance of civil behavior in public. Today, hundreds of thousands of Mainland Chinese visit Taiwan every year. And they come back saying, among other things, that Taiwan is "sooooo civil." They also note that Taiwan is more "Chinese" than the Mainland, having nurtured the traditional culture all the while Mao and the Communists were doing all they could do to eradicate it on the Mainland. The Mainland is now playing catch up, trying to recover the former glory of Chinese culture. And that is good. And, with time, the Mainland will also overcome the chaos that is engendered by the lack of citizen to citizen civility. Like Taiwan, it's the pocketbook and a steady stream of public education messaging that will do the trick.

It can be argued that Confucianism should, by its very nature, exert negative influence on any attempt to implement democracy in a Chinese society. With its core starting point of authoritarian, imperial rule, it is common sense that Confucianism brings this fly in the ointment to the table. It is no small challenge to overcome, and partially explains why Chinese are so vulnerable to becoming followers of large political movements led by tyrants. That's where Dr. Sun Yat-sen entered the picture with his republican revolution in 1911.

Dr. Sun & The Three Principles of the People

Fortunately for the Chinese people, Dr. Sun was a leader who understood the limitations of China's culture in relation to its needed drive for nationalism and modernism. On the heels of the 1911 Revolution, Dr. Sun founded the Republic of China, which is the surviving political entity on Taiwan, led by Sun's party the Kuomintang, or Nationalist Party. Like Confucius, Dr. Sun was a target of Communist wrath during the Mao era, even though both the Communist Party and Nationalist Party owe their ideological roots to the revolution led by Dr. Sun. And, like Confucius today, Dr. Sun has also been undergoing a revival on the Mainland, mainly because the philosophy he espoused for balancing China's old culture with the developmental needs of the modern nation-state is increasingly relevant to Chinese Communist rule.

An overview of Dr. Sun's revolutionary tenets is critical to the understanding of how a blueprint for China's national development occurred on Taiwan, and how it is being imitated today on the Chinese mainland. You will find that Dr. Sun's "Three Principles of the People," his teachings on how China should develop into a modern nation-state, were amazingly prescient not only as a blueprint for China's development, but with much relevance to the developing world as a whole.

Dr. Sun delivered a series of lectures in 1924 that embodied his views on how China should develop in the modern era. These lectures are known as The Three Principles of the People, standing for Nationalism, Democracy (People's Sovereignty) and The People's Livelihood. These lectures are invaluable to our understanding of how China can best reconcile its great culture with the need to form a prosperous, strong, modern nation. Dr. Sun was actually the perfect person to lead this movement, due to his upbringing in both Eastern and Western environments. A medical doctor by trade, he preferred scientific study in general, and sought to apply scientific principles to the notion of national development. Along the way, he spent much time in British H.K., and in Hawaii and Europe, striving to grasp the best of East and West thought and best practices to write a blueprint for China's national development. His works brilliantly outlined how developing states with old cultures could navigate their way to achieving modern development, and thus have as much relevance today as they did back in his day.

Just at the time Sun was studying the various political, social and economic models of both the Eastern and Western traditions, the world was undergoing a period of tremendous struggle among competing ideologies. Marxism gaining popularity, and the first communist state, the Soviet Union, was newly established. Dr. Sun happened to be in Europe when Marxism began to collide with Capitalism, so he was getting an up close and personal snapshot of the thought trends of the day. China was still mostly feudal so Sun sought to find either the right balance for China or a totally new path for it to follow.

The Principle of Nationalism

His starting point was Nationalism. For hundreds of years China had been the victim of foreign domination and humiliation. The disastrous Boxer Rebellion of 1900 taught Sun early on that China needed to extricate itself from the mire of foreign domination first, before it could ever entertain any serious thought to how it might develop the trappings of the modern nation-state internally.

Interestingly, however, Sun did not lay all the blame on foreigners for China's abject weakness and image as the "sick man of Asia." Like many other modern Chinese thinkers, Sun wrestled with the fact that China had once been at the pinnacle of human civilization, but had gradually over hundreds of years lost its leading position, ending up at the turn of the 20th Century at the bottom of the heap not only in terms of prestige, but also in the dour reality of poverty and backwardness. In his first lectures on Nationalism, Sun spent much time arguing that China's weakness was also the result of not having developed a spirit of nationalism. Over the millennia, the clan was the dominant concern. Add to this the "blinder" effect of a strong homogeneous culture, and you had the makings of failure, according to Sun. He put forth the notion that the nation and the culture were two separate things, and that if Chinese continued to rely solely on their culture for progress, they would ultimately continue to fail to enter the ranks of modern nation-states. Only by emphasizing nationalism, or a spirit of national unity, could China throw off not only the shackles of foreign domination, but also those things which held them back from within. He also made the points that foreigners would continue to treat China as what he called a "hypo-colony," (domination by many foreign states), incapable of "awakening and governing itself."

Sun used his lectures on Nationalism to educate Chinese about the need to move beyond clanism and toward nationalism as a means of national salvation. In his time, China was teetering on the abyss of extinction, and would end up like Egyptian culture which was lost to the world. He advised that China had to become more nationalistic so as to save its culture. He deemed it the principle of Nationalism to be the first step needed to ensure the perpetuation of all things Chinese.

Astutely, Sun knew that the need for nationalism was not just about ridding the country of political (military) domination. It was also a necessity for ending economic domination of China by the foreign powers. He was an early proponent of ending the tariffs and other instruments of foreign economic imperialism imposed on China.

The subject of imperialism was also central to Sun's lectures on Nationalism. During his time, the Western

Powers began espousing the concept of "cosmopolitanism," or what today we call "globalism." But Sun saw through it as a ruse to make excuses for imperialism under the guise of "one world fellowship."

Sun believed that Nationalism, if properly addressed, would not be such a great challenge for the Chinese given their cultural inclination to look out for the common good and to accept certain rules of conformity to make it work. He strongly felt that the cultural bias of the Chinese people could be turned into a spirit of nationalism that would be equally powerful.

But Sun was not himself entirely cultural-centric. He also understood that China's success in building a modern nation would depend on her ability to adopt some of the best practices of the West, and certainly her technology. Economically speaking, China would not have a prayer of making progress without bringing Western technology and industrial means into the picture. This is where his background in the West was most helpful in the formulation of his views for a blueprint of national development. This entailed overcoming the residual archaic notion among many Chinese that China was still the apex of human civilization and superior to the barbarians. This cultural bias obviously flew in the face of the apocalypse that China was facing in the early part of the 20th Century. And Sun would have his work cut out for him in educating people to come around to a more mundane view of China's overall condition and what was needed to improve it.

He was uplifted by the overall trend in the world away from autocracy and toward democracy, and saw that China should go with this revolutionary flow not only for the purpose of entering the same current as the West, but also to preclude division at home. He looked forward to the day that the "king" in China would be hundreds of millions of people, and not a weak emperor unable to deal properly with the outside world. Those days would begin to come to an end with the implementation of the principle of Nationalism. The world, he predicted, would find it much less desirable to pick on a united four hundred million Chinese (it's a billion-five now, and lo and behold, few nations are picking on China these days!).

The Principle of Democracy (or People's Sovereignty)

This is an area where Dr. Sun's teachings are in need of serious re-visitation by world leaders. A man of science with a wonderful balance of Eastern and Western political philosophy, Sun laid out clearly the differences between the Western view of human rights and democracy and that of the Chinese, or East. And there are big differences.

Essentially, Westerners have grown accustomed to viewing certain civil rights as the most basic of human rights. These include suffrage, protest, and fear from government. But in the Chinese view, basic human rights start with food, clothing and shelter. Civil or political rights are way down the list of priorities, and are not God-given but rather privileges granted by the state, whether that state is representative of the people or not. Sun went out on a limb in 1924 to argue that both the French and American revolutions were based on faulty notions that confused civil rights with human rights. He also determined that the Franco-American notion of equality was seriously flawed, in that people are indeed NOT born equal but are subject to the laws of nature embodied in the human genome. Instead, Sun argued that equality should be viewed as something bestowed upon the people, by the people, in a perfect world. In the real world, equality is often forced upon society. Either way, it is not, as the first line of the American Declaration of Independence naively posits, a God-given right. Nor is it ever truly attainable according to Sun, since people are created differently according to their genes. It is telling that Sun saw the fallacy of the line "all men are created equal" and thus did not fall in step with it. The American founding fathers probably meant that line as an expression of an aspiration, and not fact. Or, as many argue, it was just in the context of their times, and can be excused that way. In any case, Sun was quite astute to call out the Americans on this flaw in their democracy. He was right to frame it in political terms, which limit it to the whims of man and not a deity.

Besides differences on human rights, Sun also noted the East and West generally did not agree on the true meaning of liberty. Westerners tend to confuse liberty with democracy, assigning too much importance to the latter at the expense of the former.

Sun believed that Chinese did not really comprehend the meaning of the word liberty, since it basically means the ability to move about as one wishes. If that is the basic definition, then Chinese considered themselves free, and had for centuries, according to Sun. It was not a matter of liberty, but one of sovereignty for the Chinese. Chinese were used to being free in the Western sense of the word, but they had yet to find a system of government that would bestow sovereignty upon them, so that they could determine their fate, free or not. Thus, Sun felt that liberty develops as the power of the people, or the true sovereigns, develops.

Sun also was critical of the French philosopher Rousseau, whose writings inspired the French Revolution. Rousseau, too, argued in his treatise SOCIAL CONTRACT that Nature bestows rights and privileges to the people, including the right to democracy. Sun rejected that notion feverishly, instead calling democracy a goal that needed much in the way of nurturing before it could take root and succeed. In his lectures, Sun noted how long it took for France to reach a truly democratic state following the revolution, with the same argument applied to other states in Europe and the United States as well. If democracy were a natural right, Sun posited, why would it be so unnatural a process to implement it?

Thus it is that while Sun was clear about democracy's pitfalls, he nevertheless espoused it as a critical long-term element needed for China's rise to modernity. This is because he could think of no other way to express the will of the people or to make the people the nation's sovereign. He adopted the Western notion of sovereignty lying with the people, and admired Lincoln for pushing this concept forward more than any other leader in the past.

In his lectures, Sun also dwelt much on the subject of the debates between the Hamilton and Jeffersonian factions in the U.S. during formulation of the nation's Constitution and form of Government. Hamilton believed in a strong federal government with many centralized powers. Jefferson opposed that view, arguing instead that the federal Government's powers should be limited, and that more power should be concentrated in the States, who would be closer to representing the people, thus giving the people more direct power of their governments. Jefferson had placed much faith in the people, who would be relied upon to exercise their newfound powers with wisdom. Hamilton considered that a recipe for disaster.

Sun recognized the validity of certain points in both arguments. And after weighing that epic battle of great minds in America with the fact that the French Revolution was followed by a period of tremendous social upheaval, Sun opted to seek a balance in China's blueprint for democratic development. Perhaps the greatest of his contributions on the subject, Sun put forth a plan that would see a long period of tutelage on democracy in China. Rather than install democracy right on the heels of the Revolution in China, and risk further breakdown and even total melt down of the Chinese state, Sun spoke out often on the need for Chinese to learn democracy gradually, perhaps starting at the grassroots and working up from there. Sun correctly estimated that an ancient culture such as China's could not possibly absorb Western democracy, for a myriad of reasons. Lack of education and literacy chief among these. He feared that a few hundred million illiterate Chinese could be adversely manipulated by competing interests in a democratic environment, and that it would be best to implement democracy only after the scourge of illiteracy was eradicated. This way the people could understand their responsibilities with regard to democratic participation, rather than just thinking of suffrage and political participation as mere rights. This view is not unlike that of the American founding fathers, who devised a system for authoritarian style democracy because they did not trust the under classes, slaves and women to participate in the affairs of government. Sun advocated a period of democratic tutelage, but did not know how long that process would take.

The other reason Sun urged caution in adopting democracy in China was because the practice was still relatively new in the West. That is, true democracy. Europe still had kings, and the U.S. had only recently given suffrage to half its population (women in 1920), so Sun considered democracy greatly untested, even if he saw it as the logical world trend following thousands of years of theocracy and autocracy. The history of democracy, especially in the periods following revolutions that brought it about, showed that true democracy was not achieved until much later on. In fact, Sun places much emphasis on the later introduction of Recall & Referendum rights in Western systems, which effectively give the people real power over their government thru post-election checks and balances. Sun, then, was essentially arguing that China should not imitate the result of Western democratic progress, but rather the process in getting there. That is essentially a core position of this book.

He also cautioned Westerners to understand up front that Chinese democracy would eventually take on its own characteristics, and probably not imitate the West lock, stock and barrel. He said that democracy is not like machinery or technology, which can be imported and used without undermining either culture or nationalism. Democracy involved the changing of deeply rooted philosophies and tenets imbedded in China's long-lived culture. Such change, or adaptation, would certainly require much time, education and trial. Leading the cause of Nationalism at the time, Sun definitely saw this as doable, and taught that the Chinese version would someday be superior to that of the West, thanks to China's likely combination of Confucian thought and Western practice.

In his fifth lecture on democracy, given on March 16, 1924, Sun touched on a very interesting irony of Western democracy: That the more democratic a nation becomes, the more opposed to government the people become. If the goal was to make the people sovereign via democracy, then why would they eventually oppose that which they created themselves? Hmm. This thought, generated nearly a hundred years ago, seems to ring truer today than back then! The answer probably lies in empowerment. People increasingly feel they have a stake in government because governments are becoming so large and overbearing, making many feel an increased obligation to play the role or watchdog. I dunno.

Sun asserted in the same lecture that he had come up with a new method to solve this dilemma. He argued that a distinction needed to be made between sovereignty and ability. In other words, democracy could only work if it were "managed" by the intellectual class, or those with education and ability necessary to rule on behalf of others. Sound like a drift toward authoritarianism? Probably, because after all, Sun was also a Chinese! But he clarified this view later on by saying that any political movement toward democracy would necessarily entail having "discoverers" lead, followed by early adapters or "promoters" of the cause, followed lastly by those who are operators of democracy, namely the masses. This also set the pretext for his critical notion that a period of tutelage was needed, and that obviously the educated would lead the masses until such time true democratic powers could be trusted with the people, en masse. This would also eliminate the historical pattern of having leaders with all the power but no ability, instead gradually replacing that circumstance with leaders who have the ability but who are empowered by the people. Wow!

Which leads us to another of Sun's clever observations about how China should best adopt democracy.

Sun likened democracy to the automobile. Say what? Well, it's an argument that actually works. When the automobile was first introduced, chaos ruled the streets. That's because the operators (the people) had no training on how to drive. The leaders threw the car out there and said "you take it from here." Neither were there chauffeurs or mechanics in the early days, which also led to chaotic market conditions in which the operator had to perform both tasks himself. Sun said that democracy, if introduced this way, would produce similar results. Upon which he uttered one of his most notable phrases of all time: Chinese are like loose grains of sand blowing in the wind. Adopting democracy without a "user's manual" or period of training would spell total disaster for China. In his summary of this point, Sun said that only after the people made a distinction between ability (the machine) and the sovereigns (the operators of the machine), could China progress smoothly. By gradually controlling the machine through democracy, the people could eventually exercise their full sovereignty, and check the power of the state.

Sun took it a step further by arguing for the need for much experimentation before implementation. Again, this was the scientist in him. He noted in his sixth lecture that new machines, medicines and technology only reached market after long trials and experimentation. Only thus could they safely be assimilated. He figured that democracy would need similar treatment, especially since the stakes were so much higher for society.

A final area covered by Sun was the importance of the rule of law when it comes to a developing nation's ability to absorb democracy. China was not ruled by law but by relationships or connections, thanks to the Confucian tradition. It would take a gargantuan undertaking in China to gradually implement the rule of law, replacing the far less intangible system of relationships as the guiding force of civility and order in society. Sun has proved especially prescient about this. A look at China today tells the observer that Mainland China is still caught between the age-old practice of "guanxi" versus the rule of law. The latter is gaining steam, but still has a long way to go toward full maturity.

In sum, on the subject of democracy, Dr. Sun probably shared the Hamiltonian view of the need for a larger role for a more powerful central government. This becomes evident in his next series of lectures on the People's Livelihood, in which Sun clearly comes across as something of a socialist, or at least a statist.

The People's Livelihood

In the years prior to his lectures on The Three Principles of the People, Dr. Sun was, like many intellectuals of the day, buffeted by the debates raging at the time over socialism and Marxism. After leading Marxist thinkers began to break into different schools of socialist thought, Sun was even more dubious of the potential for strict socialism. The discord and competing thoughts on the subject pushed him in the direction, once again, of finding a Chinese solution to the problem. And, as with the first two principles covered here, he did indeed uncover a distinctly Chinese path to solve the issue. It is more statist in character than socialist.

Sun began by looking at Marx's interpretation of history as a constant march of material forces and how they influence society. Sun rejected that notion, instead broadening the concept to mean the overall well-being of the people, or the pursuit of livelihood or subsistence, as the chief force driving mankind's progress. In other words, Sun believed people were the masters of their fates, at all times in history, not material circumstances.

Like others, Sun observed that the Industrial Revolution was causing serious social disruption by replacing human jobs with mechanization. This directly affected the people's livelihoods, thus the mass upheavals at the turn of the 20th Century. Sun argued that in China's case, the overall issue of livelihood needed to be addressed, not just the narrow terms defined by Marx or other socialist thinkers at the time. Thus, he called the third principle "The People's Livelihood."

Sun completely separated himself from Marx on the issue of class warfare and re-distribution of wealth, which Marx advocated as a means of seeking redress for disenfranchised workers. Marx, he said, only focused on the disease, making him a pathologist, not a real doctor with solutions to the disease. Calling on his Chinese roots, Sun theorized that social progress is attained by virtue of competing forces adjusting to and complementing each other, rather than by a clash of interests as advocated by Marx. Economic interests need to be harmonized if the majority of people are to benefit from economic progress. This is a key component of the system that was created on Taiwan, and which is now taking form in Mainland China.

It is important to simplify one major belief that Sun held on capitalism. Essentially, he agreed that capitalism was necessary as the best engine for human progress. It partly went back to his notion of leaders versus followers and the natural order of the human gene pool. It was also a conclusion he made based on his own observations, and where most progress was occurring. He considered full-on socialists to be lost in their imaginations about some Utopia out there that does not exist. But he also believed that certain aspects of socialism could be adapted to the Chinese experience, mainly as a means of putting some checks and balances on capitalists.

In particular, Sun put forth three areas in which the government should play a strong role. First, he advocated an equalization of land distribution, essentially giving land to those who tilled it, with the government controlling some lands for the common good. Second, he strongly believed in capital controls by the state, so as to rein in the otherwise unwieldy machinations of bankers and capitalists. He felt some degree of regulation was needed to protect—again— the common good. And finally, Sun believed that the state should own and operate some basic industries such as the electric grid, iron and steel, shipbuilding and other large scale industries. He deemed these too critical to the nation's development and trusted that the collective wisdom of the government would better implement these on behalf of the public.

More specifically, Sun put forward four areas of strong government involvement. These included plans for social and economic reforms, nationalization of transportation and communications, direct taxation (income and sales) and the promotion of co-operative societies or unions. He posited that these would be conducted peacefully in harmony, unlike the total disruptions of society advocated by Marx. Sun basically was calling for government to have basic tools for overall guidance of the nation's economic restructuring, rather than relying on revolutionary, more violent schemes. This emphasis on stability occurs throughout his lectures on the People's Livelihood, and also set the tone later on for Taiwan's successful development.

As Sun waded through the myriad economic theories of the day, he never lost sight of the fact that the process of adaptation should be based on scientific facts and not vague theories. He also argued that the facts had to be relevant to similar observable facts in China, and not based on any peculiarities of any one foreign country.

The issue of problems between haves and have-nots proved to be easy for Sun to navigate for one simple reason: In China, just about every one was a have-not at that time! It was a matter of degree of poverty, not rich versus poor as in the West. So, rather than having to deal with the issue of wealth disparity, Sun had to devise a blueprint that would lift EVERYONE up, a sort of all boats rise with the tide solution. The main component of this solution would be an attempt to level the playing field somewhat, but not entirely, as Sun thought that would be more pie-in-the-sky than practical. Thus he laid out plans for some Government control of financial resources, all aimed at creating an environment that would create opportunities for those with ability, and not just power. To this end, Sun still trusted the capitalists and land owners to do many of the right things in using the levers of influence available to them to help contribute to not only economic progress, but social progress as well. With a minor dose of regulation, of course!

Because China was dirt poor and had very little means of production, Sun taught that the Government must have the ability to both regulate capital and promote industrial development, whether via state industries or through support to the private sector. Thus was born his particular brand of statism, or limited socialism, of the kind seen in Taiwan over the years and which is more evident today in Mainland China. China is neither here nor there on socialism. It no longer has any vestiges of communism, but neither is it a full market economy. It is somewhere, lost, in between. But this is not a bad thing. It likely means that China is on Dr. Sun's path, with a long way to go toward achieving a truly prosperous, just society.

One of the core elements of Sun's Livelihood Principle concerns food. In Sun's day, China was still very much if not nearly entirely an agricultural society. Yet it lacked the means to feed its population. Starvation was still rampant, and Sun, calling upon his medical training, lectured heavily on the types of policies and programs that would be needed to overcome this fundamental problem.

He clearly came down hard on communism as a solution. Sun recognized the inhuman nature of that system with its tendency to suck the life out of the people by making everything collective. Sun understood the basic nature of man, and realized that incentives were the cure. That is why he put forward the case of land reform, giving land to those who tilled it as a means of incentivizing them to produce more. He argued that a regime of Government policies and even farmers' rights should be implemented to see this through. Liberating the peasantry, unleashing their potential, was one side of the coin. The other was a more scientific assessment by Sun that involved seven methods for increasing production. These were: Use of machinery, use of fertilizers, rotation of crops, eradication of pests, manufacturing (food processing), transportation and alleviating the effects of natural disasters. Again, Sun was using his twin talents as an emerging political revolutionary and scientists to devise schemes for China's national development. Sun felt that the Government needed to play a role in ensuring that food production would not be simply about profit, but also for the more altruistic goal of providing all the people with sufficient dietary needs. Sun took a rare jab at capitalism in the third lecture on Livelihood when he said that the aim of capitalism is profits, while the aim of our Livelihood Principle is the "nurture of the people." With such a noble cause, he added, we "could destroy the bad elements of capitalism" in China. The Government, he insisted, had to play a role in the basics of food, clothing and shelter, and he also added a fourth one: transportation. Another example of Sun's uncanny prescience was his argument that a robust transportation system would create egalitarian growth in China, with everyone having access to the same goods and services. Indeed. That is often what you hear about the interstate highway system in America—that it created egalitarian economic growth! Sun takes this a bit further when he says, in very Chinese fashion, that if everyone contributes his lot to the whole (farmers food, workers goods, scholars thought, and government guidance) then the needs of the lot can be fulfilled.

Thus, while not a full-on socialist by any means, Sun

did understand the pitfalls and opportunities presented by capitalism, and thus devised a blueprint that drew from both emerging systems. Of particular note here is that Sun never directly supported any program having to do with welfare. Instead, his Chineseness shone through and he loathed a society in which people did not contribute to progress.

Unfortunately, Dr. Sun died before he could complete his writings on the last principle of the People's Livelihood. The full blueprint for China's development would have to rely on interpretations made by his successors, a task which fell mainly in the lap of General Chiang Kai-shek, who would take the reigns of the Nationalist Party and begin to implement the Three Principles.

Chiang's first task was national unity. He set out on a two-pronged approach in the mid-1920s aimed at defeating warlords and unifying the country, while simultaneously initializing several large scale infrastructural projects as the foundation for nation-building.

He was having some success on both fronts. And that is what prompted the Japanese to believe that the sleeping dragon was finally beginning to awaken after centuries of slumber. They invaded China in 1937, with one aim being to keep the Chinese down (Japan invaded for a similar reason in 1895).

Chiang also faced an internal rebellion, as the Soviet-backed Chinese Communist Party did not accept Sun's blueprint, instead wanting to implement Soviet-style Marxism in China as a means of overcoming China's age-old weaknesses and mass poverty. The Chinese thus fought a long hard civil war, much of it during the Japanese invasion, over a single ideal: Should China follow Marx and Communism, or Sun and Capitalism, with a dash of Socialism? Dirt poor as it was, China no doubt was fertile ground for the message of communism.

The Communists won the civil war in 1949, four years after the Japanese were defeated by the allies. That is, the Communists won the military war. But the war over the idea continued with Chiang Kai-shek's retreat to Taiwan following the Communist takeover. Not only did the Government of the Republic of China remain alive on Taiwan, but so did Sun's blueprint for a modern China. As we will discover in the next chapters, Chiang and the Nationalists went on to win the war of ideas. The successful experience they created on Taiwan now serves as the model for Mainland China's development. It has Dr. Sun Yat-sen's fingerprints all over it.

Imagine this: If the fierce rivals Chiang Kai-shek and Mao Zedong would rise from the grave, and they looked at China today, what would their respective responses be? Mao would either faint or cry for another revolution. China today resembles nothing that he envisioned, because his idea lost the war and the Mainland is now following Dr. Sun's path of development, that is to say, Chiang Ka-shek's path of development, that is to say, the Nationalists' path of development. For his part, Chiang would likely cry out, "We won! Dr. Sun, we did it!" Go figure…

7 THE TAIWAN ECONOMIC EXPERIENCE: HOW IT'S DONE

Which provides us the perfect segue to our core discussion of the Taiwan experience, and how the "economics first" model works. Development experts since the late-70s have regarded Taiwan as one of the world's most successful models of development. No other society grew so fast and so equitably as Taiwan did in the post-World War II era. And, importantly, you will see just how Dr. Sun's blueprint for China unfolded on Taiwan. It got a lot of attention for its success among scholars in the early Eighties, but the notice has petered out for some odd reason. Just when nation-building is back in vogue (thanks to George W. in Iraq and Afghanistan and continuation of the failed U.S. foreign policy of forcing the drug of democracy down the throats of unstable nations), the most successful model is forgotten or ignored. Doesn't make a lick of sense to this boy from Tippecanoe, Ohio.

One short generation goes by and everyone forgets what happened in East Asia. Good books on the subject of economic development on Taiwan are gone from the shelves. Books such as economist Shirley Kuo's THE TAIWAN SUCCESS STORY (1981). That book lays it all out for everyone to see. Plain as day. All the facts, all the figures of Taiwan's so called "miraculous" economic development. And then there's MODELS OF DEVELOPMENT, edited by Lawrence Lau, 1986. It covers Taiwan and South Korea. And for good measure, try THE TAIWAN EXPERIENCE, edited by James Hsiung, also 1981. These easy to read tomes on the Taiwan experience should be required reading in developing countries. They are primers on how to reach first the Turning Point in economic development, then the Stakeholder Society, both quickly and with egalitarian distribution of wealth.

Yet when one talks about the Taiwan experience in places like South America, people walk away, asserting cultural differences. What a cop out.

Taiwan did so much right on its path to development that it's difficult to know where to start. In writing this easy-to-read overview of the Taiwan experience, I draw heavily upon the development experts cited above.

But first, let's make sure we are all starting out on the same page with a brief glance at Taiwan's history.

A Glance at Taiwan's History

Largely ignored prior to a migration of Chinese there in the Seventeenth Century, Taiwan has since played a controversial role in geo-politics. The Portuguese were the first Westerners to "discover" the island in 1640. The Dutch took over the island in 1696, only to have Chinese, led by the pirate leader Koxinga, take it back. Chinese ruled the island with little administration emanating from the Mainland. In 1895, Japan took the island as part of its spoils in winning the first Sino-Japanese War. Taiwan remained a colony of Japan until Japan's surrender at the end of the second Sino-Japanese War in 1945, and simultaneously the end of the Second World War, when it was formally returned to the Republic of China. China, however, was embroiled in a tragic civil war that had been waged throughout Japan's occupation of the nation until 1945. The Chinese Communist Party, backed by the Soviets, was engaging the Nationalist Party, which had founded the republic in 1912 following Dr. Sun Yat-sen's rebellion against the Qing Dynasty, the last of China's nearly three thousand years of dynastic rule. In 1949, the Chinese Communists, led by Mao Zedong, overthrew the Nationalist Government, led by President Chiang Kai-shek, who then fled to Taiwan to set up a last bulwark against Communist encroachment. From 1949 to the present, the Nationalists on Taiwan and the Communists on the Mainland have existed mainly as foes, with Beijing oft repeating its assertion that Taiwan is part of historical and geographic China, and that Beijing has the right to take it back by any means it deems appropriate or necessary. Taipei, for its part, has long asserted that the Republic of China still exists on Taiwan, and that China is divided into two competing governments. China says Taiwan is a renegade Chinese province, protected by the U.S. Most interesting to note is that the one thing both sides agree on—that there is only one China and Taiwan is part of it—is the very thing that keeps them apart. Neither will concede the other's legitimacy, thus the stalemate.

In recent years, however, a major opening has occurred across the Taiwan Strait. What Chinese on both sides call the "Three Contacts," has yielded incredible results for not only cross-Strait cooperation but also for the economic well-being of the two sides. When openings first occurred in the mid-90s, Taiwan quickly became the largest investor in the Mainland (and is to this day—still some forty percent of China's export volume is coming from Taiwan owned or joint venture factories on the Mainland). In an unfortunate twist, the Nobel Prize Committee decided to give the 2009 Peace Prize to U.S. President Barack Obama (why, no one could understand), when in fact, the leaders of Taiwan and the Mainland should have got credit for their world-changing peace-building efforts across the Taiwan Strait!

For purposes of clarity, it is important to note here that I am on the side that asserts Taiwan is part of historical and geographic China and that the separation is artificial and will work out a political solution eventually. I do not buy into the claims of those Taiwanese who clamor for independence from China, permanently. The de facto independence of the past seventy years should not be considered the basis for permanent separation., in my view. I tend to take the view of my Father-in-law, a native born Taiwanese who was staunchly pro-Nationalist and would never have thought of Taiwan as not being part of China. I am in the majority of Taiwanese on this subject. While there is a vocal minority on the island, when push comes to shove, a vast majority of Taiwan Chinese favor either the status quo or unification over independence. Independence is, after all, a totally dead end path given that Beijing says it will not accept such a declaration and the U.S., among other powers, has said it will not support such a declaration.

Taiwan has fared well all these years under the status quo of one China, two governments. Typical of Chinese, both sides of the Strait have put economics ahead of politics, and are letting economic relations lead the way toward what many assume will be a long slow process toward some sort of unification (if China can hold itself together!). More on that later…

In the meantime, when it comes to the subject of nation-building per se, I do refer to Taiwan as a nation, but only in the context of it being an example for other nations to follow. In reality, and in a perfect world, I consider Taiwan to be a province of China. But the de facto status quo, as it is, argues the case for Taiwan as a nation-state as well. It fits the definition in terms of its long-term control over a territory, having official relations with other nations (some 15 nations still recognize the Republic of China on Taiwan as the official government of China, like the U.S. did up until 1979, and the Japanese did until 1972). Taiwan's democracy also qualifies it for nationhood under several instances of international jurisprudence. That aside, I still stick with the majority Chinese narrative, both on Taiwan and in the Mainland, that Taiwan is an inalienable part of historic, geographic China.

With that background, let's get on with our review of what has made Taiwan so successful.

Post Civil War Taiwan

It all goes back to 1949-50. That is the year Chiang Kai-shek and the Nationalists were driven from China by the Communists, led by that Economics Hall of Shame genius, Mao Zedong.

When Chiang arrived on Taiwan with his rag tag military in tow, the island was devastated by years of World War and struggling with civil conflict over its very identity. As noted earlier, the Japanese had ruled Taiwan as a colony since 1895, when Taiwan was ceded to Japan as one of the spoils of Japan's first conquest of China. The Japanese controlled politics on the island, but did manage to begin creating a solid infrastructure on the island. Much of that was destroyed by war, but enough of it was around for the infrastructure to be somewhat of a key in Taiwan's latter economic take-off.

Chiang faced a real dilemma on Taiwan. When the island was returned to China (The Nationalists) in 1945, Chiang was too busy fighting the civil war with the Communists to do much about Taiwan. The islanders at first rejoiced (in general) about their return to the Motherland. But joy soon turned to a realization that they were being neglected. Chiang was tied down on the Mainland, and treated Taiwan like a red-headed step child. Resentments grew. Protests broke out around the island,

and when Chiang did turn his attention to the island, it was for ill. He allowed a cruel governor, Chen Yi, to stamp out the protests with force. Many were killed, especially in a February 28 incident in 1948. Taiwanese sentiments began to turn against the Nationalists, who were now increasingly viewed as conquerors rather than saviors.

By the time Chiang and the Nationalist Government arrived en masse from the Mainland in 1949, Taiwan was a mess. It was dirt poor. Its per capita income was under $70. The people felt betrayed. The Communists were telling the world that they were coming for Taiwan. Things could not have looked any worse.

But the tide soon changed. Two things happened to turn it. First, the *fluke* that saved Taiwan occurred. Mao's forces were building up steam in men and materials to invade Taiwan in early 1950. As the storm gathered on the Mainland side, and fears grew on the Taiwan side, a little creature decided to play its hand in the fate of a nation. The river fluke. Tiny little guy with big results. The river fluke decimated Mao's invasion force. So rampant was the sickness that Mao had to call off the invasion of Taiwan indefinitely. Thus, it became known as the fluke that saved Taiwan.

Which provided enough time for the second event that combined to save Taiwan. In a rare show of commitment to stop the Communist advance, President Truman ordered the U.S. Seventh Fleet into the Taiwan Strait. This was in 1952, following the outbreak of hostilities on the Korean peninsula. It was there that Truman finally decided to draw the line on the worldwide Communist advance. Suddenly, Taiwan became a key player again in U.S. foreign policy. I personally thank Truman for that move, but I still have not forgot nor forgiven him for the fact that half the world became Communist on his watch. Oh, those little remembered facts about wonderful Harry! How great he was. A great friend of Stalin and Mao, that is. Until he saved Taiwan.

The third thing that helped save Taiwan was Chiang Kai-shek's stunning economic policies on the island. In 1950, Taiwan was dirt poor, just like the rest of the developing or underdeveloped world (formerly known as the Third World). Its per capita income was close to zilch, but really around USD$70 a year. Children were barefoot. Just another poor place wallowing in war-torn poverty.

That all changed dramatically with the introduction of two of the important keys to Taiwan's overall development: The Social Compact and Land Reform. These are separate but equal as the foundations of Taiwan's economic miracle. Later on, more elements were introduced, and by 1979, Taiwan had reached the status of what I call a STAKEHOLDER SOCIETY, or what economists have traditionally referred to as the Turning Point in economic development. That's when a nation officially joins the First World. Taiwan had reached a per capita income of $12,000. In a short 25 years, it had gone from the embarrassment of poverty to an embarrassment of riches. Only there is nothing embarrassing at all about following brilliant economic policies and putting economics ahead of politics to achieve those riches.

When the Nationalist Government moved to Taipei in 1949, the island was war-torn and restless. There had been some progress on the island after it was returned to the Republic of China by Japan in 1945. Much of the war damage to the infrastructure was repaired. Indeed, it needs to be noted that the infrastructure left behind by the Japanese was fairly substantial and certainly provided a foundation for the economic growth that was about to occur on Taiwan.

The Nationalists were faced with the immediate problem of how to combat the appeal of communism to dirt poor people. It needed to quickly devise the plans for raising incomes and increasing the people's livelihoods. This was a key issue in the Chinese civil war, and key to Dr. Sun's blueprint for development, as we have seen.

The Nationalists correctly surmised that addressing the issue of equitable income growth and distribution was Job #1. But to succeed, they would have to blaze a new path for development, and reject models of that day that had led to some rapid growth in the developing world, but with the resultant burden of huge gaps in incomes between rich and poor. That was far from desirable for a government that not only had a score to settle with the Communists over the Big Idea, but who were also under tremendous pressure to deliver on the social compact they would offer the Taiwan Chinese.

In existing models of development, rapid growth caused that large disparity in incomes, and it meant waiting around for equity to catch up with the income growth. It rarely did, so Taiwan wanted to create a new model that would both alleviate the political pressures and raise incomes dramatically. A focus on equitable growth would be the only way to tackle both concerns at the same time. There were not many rich persons in Taiwan in 1950, but there was a landlord class in the agricultural sector that needed to be dealt with. So, the Government devised a set of plans that would greatly raise the incomes of the poor while not adversely affecting the rich.

It all worked wonders. From 1952 to 1979, Taiwan averaged 9.2% economic growth. Income went from $70 per capita per annum to $2,280 by 1980. Real GNP doubled every year after 1963. The society shifted dramatically from its former reliance on agriculture to an urbanized, industrial one, even while agricultural sector incomes and output continued to rise year after year. The sector dropped from 32% of the GDP to 9% of GDP in 1979, but as a whole, the sector had multiplied many times over in size. That fact alone tells you just how dramatic Taiwan's industrial growth was.

To catalyze such growth, the Nationalists started with the Social Compact, and immediately began to implement policies that would ensure deliverance on their side of the bargain. These included four main programs to set the stage:

The first was reforms of Monetary Policy. Hyper-inflation in the post-War period was off the charts, reaching as much as 500% at times. To get a handle on this, the Government de-valued the Taiwan dollar by creating a

New Taiwan Dollar, which remains the currency today. It was devalued 40,000 times, if you can imagine that! Meanwhile, the Government controlled the gold market, and moved to create a very conservative reserve system. These policies worked slowly to tackle inflation and bring monetary flow under control, and within ten years the whole system was solidly stable. Note that this emphasis on financial controls was a main pillar of Dr. Sun's blueprint for early development.

The second program was Interest Rate Controls. In 1950, the Government implemented a hugely liberal Preferential Interest Rate program that offered annual rates of as much as 125%! Rates of 7% per month were also common. This encouraged savings early on, and the national savings rate later became one of the chief hallmarks of Taiwan's development. The island enjoyed one of the top two or three rates of savings in the world, along with Japan.

The third immediate program concerned the Government Budget. It was decided early on that no matter what, fiscal conservatism would be the rule. There would be no tolerance for budget deficits. On this subject, I can share an anecdote I learned from Mr. Yu Kuo-hwa, who was the long-time head of Taiwan's Central Bank before becoming Premier in the early Eighties. I often worked with Yu on white papers and speeches, and one day I asked him why it had taken Taiwan so long to start spending huge sums on national infrastructure projects, when the island had the money to do it years earlier. Yu responded in a fashion typical of his generation in China: He said that the

Chinese people had been poor since time immemorial, and now that one province in China had become rich, it was not about to squander the wealth just to show off. He was referring somewhat to nations in the Middle East who had been spending fortunes to build palatial public structures. This story left an indelible mark on my understanding of the Chinese mind when it comes to financial issues. I was also getting a daily earful of this from my mother-in-law in Taipei, who was so fiscally conservative (though well off) that she would call up her kids and ask them if it were okay if "Mama bought herself a jade pendant!"

But the one area Taiwan could NOT scrimp by on with national budget was defense. That sector took up nearly 50% of Government spending all the way up until recent times, mainly because back in the day the Communists held a press conference every day in Beijing telling the world that they reserved the right to invade Taiwan at their pleasure. There was no ignoring that threat, given that the Mainland is 240 times bigger than Taiwan with 60 times the population. And just think: What would Taiwan's spectacular, world-leading growth had been like if freed from the burden of a national defense budget that took up half of all public monies for four decades??? It's almost unimaginable what Taiwan could have achieved.

The fourth program undertaken in the pre-1950 time frame was Foreign Exchange Reform. The Government kept firm control over it, but still implemented policies that were considered liberal for the day. It managed the exchange rate with the U.S. dollar, rather than let it float freely, throughout the early development in the 1950s.

Together, these financial reforms set the stage for the major piece of economic reform that became the true hallmark of Taiwan's overall success—Land Reform.

The keys to Taiwan's success should be understood and propagated throughout the developing world. Folks should ignore Washington, and focus on real, relevant models of nation-building.

The following is a step-by-step look at how Taiwan developed, so quickly, so equitably. I keep the narrative light and breezy so as to keep you from getting bogged down in economic theory and piles of data. This is a story that is best told as a story. Let the academics do the anti-insomniac piece of it. There are six main Acts in the Taiwan story. Here they are.

ACT ONE: THE SOCIAL COMPACT

Bottom line folks. This is the real key to development. Without it, there is no pot of gold at the end of the rainbow. And for that matter, no stable democracy, either.

If Chiang Kai-shek deserves credit for any facet of Taiwan's development, it's this one. His back against the wall, the Communists threatening to invade every day, and five years of resentment built up among the Taiwanese over their past neglect at the hands of the Nationalists, Chiang had little choice but to be quick on his feet with fast, meaningful solutions. A big one came.

Rather than crush the Taiwanese with force, he offered

them the best carrot of all time: A social compact in which the Government would hold onto the lion's share of political power in exchange for providing the masses with the means of pulling their families out of poverty. Those means were economic policies aimed at unleashing the pent up entrepreneurial spirit of the locals. These included policies that might be seen as libertarian even today. The folks were basically free to pursue their economic livelihoods as they saw fit, and the Government provided them with the policy incentives to do so. Implicit in the Compact was the aspiration to turn Taiwan into a model for all of China to follow someday, preferably sooner than later. Chiang considered the civil war unfinished business, and he still had a chance to show that nation-building principles of the Republic's Founder, Dr. Sun, could still be proven out. Keep in mind here that the Chinese civil war was fought over one idea, and one idea alone: Which system would deliver China from poverty—Soviet style Communism or Dr. Sun Yat-sen's system founded on freedom and market oriented principles, with a touch of socialism? Mao and the Communists won the military conflict over the idea. But, as we shall see later, it is perfectly debatable on who has actually won the war over the idea. I have no doubts who won.

While Chiang offered up tangible means to quiet the unrest and give people hope, his nemesis Mao was busy turning Mainland China into the largest gulag of all time. While Chiang pressed forward with the goal of implementing Dr. Sun's blueprint for raising the people's livelihood and creating an equitable society, Mao harshly implemented policies that crushed economic activity and enslaved the people. True, everyone would end up equal in Communist China (except for Communist leaders)—it's just that everyone ended up equally POOR.

But Taiwan's social compact would soon turn out to be one of the most successful in human history. Everyone from the Romans on up failed at it. But Chiang and the Nationalists pushed the right buttons.

The social compact on Taiwan is terribly important to understand. On the one hand, the Government knew that the Taiwanese were tired of poverty. It knew the people would put the welfare of their families first. And that's basically what happened on the island. The Taiwanese agreed, en masse, with few radical exceptions, to accept Chiang's offer of trading political rights for full steam ahead economic rights. What good was democracy if you had no food to eat? Or could not clothe your kids? The Taiwanese figured that one out early on. Thank goodness for that bit of awesome, and collective, wisdom garnered over the millennia by the Chinese.

To be sure, some Taiwanese resisted. But only a handful of bleeding heart liberals. There's some in every bunch. Neptunians love them for their totally irrational view of economics. To a liberal, it's always been more important to have the right to climb the fence of a nuclear power plant in protest than it is to have the right to have electricity at all. The overwhelming majority of Taiwanese got it, though. The Government could go play politics all it wanted so long as it stayed out of the way of business, or at the very least, kept coming up with policies that were conducive to free business.

And there's that freedom word again. The Taiwanese understood the difference between being democratic and being free. They are not one and the same, and never have been. If only the presidents Bush had figured that out! It sounds a bit counterintuitive at first, but think about it. The Taiwanese were free economically, and raised themselves up with that freedom. Their political freedom came later, AFTER they had established the very rationale (THE STAKEHOLDER SOCIETY!) for moving to that next phase of their development. Thus, freedom was the foundation of Taiwan's development, not democracy. Give people great amounts of economic freedom, and they do great things. Give them great amounts of democracy when they are not ready for it and the nation is not ready for it, and they get stupid. They get mired in the sandbox of politics. The Taiwanese wisely JUST SAID NO TO DEMOCRACY and got on with the business of using their newfound economic freedoms to get what they really wanted: Prosperity for their future generations. They threw off the shackles of poverty and disease with economic freedom as their weapon, not democracy. Had they opted for democracy, they would be as poor as The Philippines or Vietnam are today.

All developing nations need to examine the mechanics of Taiwan's early social compact. It requires wise leadership and wiser people to pull off, to be sure. But nothing beats an agreement between the government and the people that aims to end the incessant cycle of poverty, civil war and disease. The Taiwan model clearly shows that such a social compact based on maintaining social stability can lead to economic success. With one key caveat, of course: the Government MUST deliver on its side of the compact. You know free people who are beginning to prosper as never before will deliver on their side of the bargain. The key is the Government's promise to be a good steward of the nation's eventual march to full-blown, stable democracy. No mistake about this.

On Taiwan, the Government implemented a rather unique form of what became widely known as Martial Law, even though the Nationalists never implemented true military rule. They kept with civilian rule, but used the term Martial Law as a means of sending a message to their enemy across the Strait, and to potential oppositionists at home. The Martial Law in Taiwan was built upon strict security measures that kept opposition voices in check, again, for the purpose of preserving the "common good." This is a bit hard to swallow for Westerners, and I, too, struggled with it upon first arriving in Taiwan in September 1978. I was coming from the Soviet Union, so it puzzled me that a staunch U.S. ally that was clearly prosperous economically had a bit of Soviet flavor to it. But once you get past the issue of their unusual need for security, with a giant enemy on the Mainland saying everyday that it reserved the right to invade Taiwan at its own whim, then you get the picture. Put that against the backdrop of the Nationalists' commitment to implementing the full complement of Dr. Sun's Three Principles, and how they were committed to doing it no matter how gradually, and you could begin to have some faith in what was happening on Taiwan. By my departure at the end of May 1979, I certainly did.

Taiwan's brand of martial law can only be described as a benevolent form. Only a handful of dissidents over the years suffered terribly by it, but by the Chinese tradition of the common good, these "rock the boaters" were generally not accepted by the vast majority of Taiwan Chinese. The martial law was designed to keep the nation at peace and on a development path toward economic prosperity and eventual democracy. It worked. When all is said and done, and looking back in hindsight, it was worth it.

We already said that Taiwan's martial law was a strange or unique form. Another manifestation of that was the implementation of democracy at the grassroots level on the island. This, too, was a key component of the Social Compact in Taiwan. While Chiang and the Nationalists held tightly onto central government controls, they began holding free elections at the local levels on the island starting in 1953. By local, we mean local county and on the provincial level (remember, Taipei has maintained a two-layered administration of the island, one administering Taiwan as a province, one as a nation's central government). Dr. Sun had called for the incubation or experimentation with democracy at the grassroots level in what he called the Period of Tutelage. In other words, he recognized that the Chinese people needed to be educated first on democracy, before actually being given the reigns of power in a Lincolnian sense of sovereignty. Among Dr. Sun's most famous iterations is his admonition that the "Chinese are like grains of sand bowing in the wind," and are thus unsuited for democracy without first having a period of tutelage imposed on them. In the West, we say it's like herding cats. My experience tells me two things about Chinese: First, Dr. Sun was dead right about what he said, and second, the Chinese themselves will acknowledge the truth in what he said. I hear it all the time.

In sum, no discussion of the Taiwan's Social Compact is complete without understanding that the Martial Law was offset by 1) economics would be put first for the common good, and 2) democracy would not be entirely put off, and that at least at the local levels of government, the Taiwanese would gradually learn how to live with democracy in a fashion that still put the common good first.

ACT TWO: LAND REFORM

One of Chiang Kai-shek's initial brilliant moves was to surround himself with economic advisors who had great vision, and who were real risk takers. Such men as K.T. Li, C.Y. Kuo, Sun Yun-suan, Chen Cheng and Yu Kuo-hwa among others are men that need to be studied still today. They provided Chiang with the early answers to most if not all of his dilemmas, both economic and political, vis-à-vis the Taiwanese populace.

The key policy was Land Reform. This innovative measure changed Taiwan's course of development forever, and as you know, for the better. Much better. Here's how it worked:

When the Nationalists took over Taiwan, they also took over the industries left behind by the Japanese colonialists. There were four major State-owned businesses on the island. The Taiwanese, meanwhile, had largely been shut out of industry (and higher education), and were thus mainly tenant farmers, or just plain unemployed. This is what the Nationalists inherited. What they turned it into, and how they did it, is one of the greatest stories of human development ever written.

Though Land Reform is given much credit for turning Taiwan into the powerhouse it is today, it alone could not fix some of the challenges the island faced with regard to land and farming. For starters, Taiwan is an extremely rugged, mountainous island that has little in the way of arable land. Three-fourths of its population has always lived on one-fourth of the land. The geography and dense population presented challenges that would require Land Reform to be a first step toward solving economic issues.

It was supported by two important inputs from the United States: Financial aid to the agricultural sector, and the establishment of the Joint Commission of Rural Reconstruction (JCRR) in 1948. This was enacted by the U.S. Congress to provide financial aid, technical support and research to Taiwan for the purpose of supporting the Government's overall economic policies, which the U.S. found favorable, and trustworthy since the U.S. was quite familiar with the economic team surrounding Chiang Kai-shek. The JCRR turned out to be a major catalyst of reform and growth in Taiwan, and the Taiwan Chinese have always given the JCRR its proper due credit.

Land Reform on Taiwan is the umbrella name given to

a three-pronged series of programs. It was conceived for two main purposes: First, to address fairness issues in the long-standing landlord-tenants relationship, and second, to dramatically spur agricultural productivity as a means of greatly improving incomes and living standards in what was then mainly an agrarian society. Note that both of these reasons fit well the narrative of Dr. Sun's Three Principles of the People.

The three programs that made up Land Reform were: 1) Reduced Rents; 2) Public Land Sales, and 3) Land to the Tiller.

Under the Reduced Rents program, the Government sought to dramatically increase the farmer's share of crop yields. Prior to the reform, farmers generally received around 50% of yield income, with no protections for natural disasters and other negative influences on annual yields. The Government set a cap on the landlord's portion at 37.5%. It also provided new protections for the effects of natural disasters, allowing farmers to seek assistance in garnering higher percentages of the lower yields that resulted from such calamities. The Government also greatly strengthened farmers' associations and co-ops, which had been mostly top-down in nature. This system was also part of the new safety net for farmers. As a result of these initial policies, the price of farmland dropped dramatically, as incomes rose, allowing tenants to buy their own land.

Next came the Sale of Public Lands to support agricultural policy. In 1948-49, 25% of Taiwan's arable land was owned by the Government, whose previous owner was the Japanese Government. In 1948-53, 35% of that land was sold by the Government, and in 1953-58 another 43% was sold into private hands. This greatly expanded the amount of arable land available to farm families, though much of it was bought by landlords, with some by former tenants. The key point to this sell off of public lands by the Government was for Government to set an example for the final step of Land Reform, the Land to the Tiller program.

This third and final program became the hallmark of Taiwan's early development success. Scholars world wide have noted its success. The purpose of the program was two-fold: First, to encourage greater productivity by turning land over to those who tilled it, and second, it was designed as a redistribution of wealth measure. It was also thought that it would help spur industrial development since its key component was a compulsory selling of the land at artificially low prices to tenants in exchange for stocks in the four major state-owned enterprises. The opposite of what Mao was doing on the Mainland (killing or imprisoning landlords and turning the land into communes), Chiang's team on Taiwan had devised one of the most brilliant economic trade-offs in history. Many of the landlords cashed in right away by selling their stocks. Some used it to improve their lifestyles but many used the income to start small businesses. Some of those who kept their stock later became Taiwan's top industrialists.

The Land to the Tiller program also had much positive collateral effect on the island's economy (besides productivity soaring beyond imagination, thanks to the hard work of people who tilled more to make more). Among other things, it gave rise to multi-cropping and the introduction of higher yield crops and higher value crops, these moves made possible by rising farm incomes. But one of the main collateral successes was the fact that the Land to Tiller program gave farmers the tools and incentives to improve their lot just when the Government was also pushing new import substitution policies, which, in prior cases of development in other countries, had led to doom for the agricultural sector. Because Taiwan's farmers were prospering as a result of Land Reform, they were effectively shielded from this potential collateral damage to their well-being.

Land Reform also led to urban migration on the island as the farmers gradually used their new incomes to mechanize production, creating even greater productivity, but forcing employment in the sector down. Urbanization is typically seen as a good thing as it usually means incomes are rising fast enough to allow the agrarian population to shift elsewhere. In addition, the labor participation rate of women grew dramatically at this time partly due to increased work on family farms and partly due to flight to urban areas where jobs were beginning to spawn.

During the Land Reform phase, the Government also implemented some other policies that clearly had Dr. Sun's finger prints all over them. A key one was controls on the price of the island's main agricultural staple, rice. The Government controlled the price with an eye toward keeping it stable in a rapidly changing market environment.

Sugar was also controlled, but that was mainly by virtue of sugar having been one of the large state-owned enterprises. In all, this was a Government that was clearly letting market forces run their course to deliver results, but with a dash of Government intervention in areas that had direct bearing on the lives of all the people on the island. This was the kind of economic stewardship that Dr. Sun had called for as a means of looking out for the people's fundamental livelihoods.

The success of Land Reform on Taiwan cannot be underestimated. Not only did agricultural production soar, leading to vast surpluses in Taiwan, but incomes rose along side that growth, creating the kind of equity that underpinned the Government's main aspiration for the program. This was key in turning people's attention away from the inhuman system of Communism being forced by the barrel of a gun down the throats of Taiwan's compatriots on the Mainland.

And here is another VERY important point about Chiang's Land Reform: Not only did it spur production in both agriculture and industry, but as we have noted it also helped redistribute wealth without upsetting the apple cart altogether (re: Mao). Leaders today must study the Taiwan land reform as THE case study for redistributing wealth in a win-win fashion. Today's leaders seem more often than not to think that redistribution of wealth can only be achieved in a fashion that makes the poor richer by making the rich poorer. President Obama needs to seriously listen up here. Taiwan proved that you can make everyone prosper from a well-thought out system. This was a very timely blow to Marxists everywhere.

And finally, it is important to note that the huge success in the agricultural sector, which led to the affordability of mass mechanization of the farms, created tremendous pressure on urbanization and the establishment of other industries to absorb the labor. Fortunately, just as the agricultural policies were succeeding, so the light industry development began to take off. This allowed for the reallocation of labor from the farms to the industries cropping up (forgive the pun or mixed metaphor!) in more urban and coastal areas. The timing could not have been better for the convergence of these two trends.

ACT THREE: THE IMPORT SUBSTITUTION AND LIGHT INDUSTRY PHASE

During the same time that Land Reform was put into its final phases of implementation, the Nationalist Government also began to support a program of import substitutions to begin building light industry on the island. This program was receiving aid from the U.S., as the Americans at the time saw it as the next logical step in early development. Fortunately, Land Reform was generating the incomes needed to make this addition to the economy, and for its part, the U.S. provided aid and loans to enable Taiwan to create the environment for light industrial production.

As previously noted, it was the success of farm policy that created the surplus of labor that could be allocated to this new path of economic development. Labor wage rates stayed ahead of productivity growth rates in both sectors, keeping Taiwan ahead of what Professors Fei and Rains referred to as the "critical minimum effort" needed to ensure stability or even growth of incomes. Taiwan eventually reached a turning point in 1968 when labor wages exceeded productivity rates for good, which also created positive new levels of labor absorption into industry. In fact, workers' wages grew faster than white collar staff, and it was trends such as this that helped keep Taiwan's labor force content. During the Fifties and Sixties Taiwan experienced very little in the way of labor unrest, especially as contrasted with other lesser developed countries of that era.

One of the key support mechanisms for the development of light industry in Taiwan was the Government's emphasis on education. Which I will cover in the next act.

The light industry phase was characterized by investment in three main areas: Food processing, textiles and light electrical equipment/appliances. They developed in that order. Because agricultural productivity had skyrocketed so much with the Land to the Tiller program, Taiwan was producing some four times the produce it needed domestically. This gave rise to not only exports, but also the whole food processing industry on the island. Taiwan quickly became a large supplier of processed foods, and fresh fruits and vegetables, to Japan, for instance.

As food processing took off, textiles soon followed

using surplus products from the agricultural sector as well. The U.S. aid helped Taiwan finance the importation of the production machinery for both food processing and textiles, and the knowledge and experience gained from these endeavors soon spilled over to light industrial concerns, especially in the electrical sector.

By 1965, Taiwan was producing more in both the agriculture and industrial sectors than its domestic economy could absorb. Pressure built to expand to overseas markets via exports.

This led to an interesting, and at the time unusual spat between Taiwan and the U.S. Taiwan wanted to move quickly beyond import substitution and into exports. The surplus production badly needed new markets. The U.S. kept balking, relying mostly on older models of development, none of which Taiwan's economists saw as appealing or relevant. What Taiwan's leaders feared most was a stall in progress, harking back to the social compact. In the end, Taiwan decided to abruptly end the U.S. aid program and set out on its own.

It was a wise move that led to one of history's greatest explosions of economic growth and wealth-building.

ACT FOUR: EDUCATION AND SOCIAL POLICY

Although not economic policies per se, there were three other key contributors to Taiwan's economic success that drew from social policy. These are a heavy emphasis on education, universal healthcare and no welfare system.

In all three of these endeavors Taiwan can be shown to have set some of the best examples in the world.

EDUCATION

One of the key support mechanisms of the development of light industry in Taiwan was the Government's emphasis on education. Throughout 1950 to 1965, education accounted for a whopping 13% of the national budget. Under Japan, Taiwan Chinese were mostly only accorded primary school educations, with only a handful allowed to go on to higher education, mainly in medicine. Under the Nationalists, this changed dramatically in the early Fifties with the introduction of a 12-year education system that included compulsory primary schooling. In 1968, education was elevated once again with the introduction of a 9-year compulsory system, and implementation of low tuitions and entrance exams to high school and university level studies to ensure a level playing field for rich and poor. It was Taiwan's investment in vocational schools, however, that contributed most to the island's dramatic development of industries. English was required, and as foreign OEM investors later learned into the Sixties, there was simply no substitute for a literate factory worker who could read manuals. Taiwan was definitely breaking new ground in the developing world, and its education policies were a major contributing factor. This emphasis on education clearly has roots in Confucian thought and the national development blueprint set forth by Dr. Sun. For Confucius, education was not really a means but an end to itself. Man was supposed to seek higher knowledge constantly, for the sake of having lots of knowledge. Respect for education is thus deeply rooted in Chinese culture, and explains why there are so many Chinese "tiger moms" out there. Children are essentially asked to make great sacrifices during their early days so as to meet the competition head on, to get ahead. Indeed, both Taiwan and the Mainland are known for the fierceness of competition in their respective systems. Kids are required to cram long hours after the school day has ended. Not to do so may mean not passing a high school or college entrance exam and being relegated to the vocational class (though, today of course, entrepreneurialism is going full steam in all areas of China, so education is not necessarily the sole path to riches that it once was). In Taiwan's case, there was no substitute for an educated workforce, and the results continue to stun the world as Taiwan is always at the top or near the top of the list of education systems around the world, based on test scores, percentages of students who go on to higher education, and so forth.

NO TO THE WELFARE STATE

This subject could be a good sequel to JUST SAY NO TO DEMOCRACY. But this is an area where culture matters, and the enduring close-knit nature of the Chinese family remains the safety net for nearly all individuals who may be handicapped and unable to work, or those who are simply down on their luck and look to family support as a bridge to what comes next. One thing is for sure: Another important aspect of Chinese culture is that being a bum is never tolerated, by the family or the society-at-large.

When I first arrived in Taipei in September 1978, there was still a handful of beggars to be seen on certain sidewalks around town. But very few, specially when contrasted with the rest of the lesser developed world at that time. By 1984, there were virtually no beggars anywhere in Taiwan.

The fact that Taiwan did not need a welfare system throughout its early development plays importantly in the island's success. And, while the oldest of Confucian traditions had much to do with it, in which the family unit operated as the safety-net for individuals down on their luck or with handicaps, the advantage of full employment rates into the Sixties and beyond cannot be underestimated. With both agriculture and industry going full on after the mid-Fifties, employment was not an issue. Taiwan was making a successful, dramatic shift from an agrarian society to an industrialized one, but still with a prosperous agriculture sector. Government budgets during these periods of rapid growth contained very little in the way of what we normally think of as welfare. It is critical to note here that this lack of a need for a welfare system is one of the things that separates the Taiwan experience from that of say, the Latin Americans, whom we've already seen bog themselves down with over-reliance on welfare states. This may be construed as a cultural difference, but in fact, having policies in place to create near full employment was probably more important a factor to Taiwan's success. The Latins could certainly find their way, along this model, also.

NATIONAL HEALTH INSURANCE

When the United States started thinking more seriously under the Obama Administration about going toward a single-payer system (Government Healthcare), it probably looked inward for solutions. It certainly doesn't appear to have examined some of the more successful systems around the globe, such as Taiwan and New Zealand. Critics would argue that these two countries are too small to be viable healthcare models, but that is bunk. It's just an excuse to blind oneself with the belief that America can always do something better.

As Americans are now learning, healthcare is a large chunk of any nation's economic activity, estimated in the case of the U.S. to be around one-sixth of the economy. It would seem the Nationalists on Taiwan clearly understood this from day one.

Taiwan today has a full-blown national healthcare system that covers everyone. And premiums remain incredible low. I am familiar with it because my wife has maintained her dual citizenship with Taiwan and she is in the healthcare system there (we also have our own private plan in the USA, but long-term it looks like Taiwan is a better bet for us).

Taiwan started out in the Fifties with what they still call Lao Bao, or employer health insurance. Government workers carry Gong Bao, which means public sector healthcare. These two insurance plans covered everyone on the island who was employed, though employees would also carry children or anyone else they wanted to place on their policy for protection. These two systems worked well into the Nineties, but then when unemployment began to raise its ugly head, the Government acted to go to a full-blown single-payer system known as Quan Min Jian Bao (All the People's Healthcare). All along the care in Taiwan has been well above international standards. In my own observation, shared by just about every Taiwanese I know, the quality of care is so-so at the street or clinic level, but is recognized as among the tops in the world for catastrophic care, such as neurological and cardiopulmonary surgery, and so on. My own experience bears that out, having lived on the island for more than 20 years. I found if you had a cold or flu, the care was robotic: Take these eight pills and go home. Unfortunately, doctors in Taiwan receive under the table kickbacks for being drug merchants, so it always riled me but never surprised me that I took home eight pills for every cold I had. But on the flip side, I know plenty of examples where people had major heart surgery, brain surgery and the like and came out of it good as new. In my humble view, my own Taiwan experience taught me that a system that looks after your catastrophic needs is really all that's needed. For the little stuff, just pay the doctor and move on. In Taiwan, the healthcare system is amazingly cheap, and that goes for premiums, deductibles and bills. This is because the Government regulates it so. In addition, one of the other hallmarks of Taiwan's system is that you DEFINITELY can choose your own doctor and hospital, ALL the time. Every hospital and clinic is in the national system, so you choose where to go and the insurance takes it from there.

The point here is that the Nationalists built a very good system early on and it saw the island through its rapid growth period, contributing for sure to the overall stability of the society-at-large. Unlike in the socialist countries of Europe, the Taiwan system is not showing any tendency toward bankruptcy, and will likely continue on as another area in which the world can learn from the Taiwan Experience.

ACT FIVE: EXPORT PROMOTION ERA

In 1965, with the island literally bursting at the seams with over-capacity and surpluses both in industrial and agricultural sectors, the Nationalist Government began implementing a broad range of policies aimed at supporting the development of export markets. In other words, the successes of policies to date had created the need for new measures to keep the ball rolling in the right direction toward prosperity and equity.

Like Japan, Taiwan had few if any natural resources, and needed to rely on imports of raw materials and machinery so as to produce finished products for markets abroad. Only in this way could the excess capacity in production be absorbed into the marketplace. In the 1950s and early Sixties, Taiwan had racked up trade deficits because it was importing raw materials, capital intensive equipment and oil. The U.S. financial aid helped cover the deficits. Prior to 1961, the U.S. aid accounted for nearly all of the foreign investment on the island.

But something had to give by 1965. It was then that Taiwan started racking up trade surpluses, even without the factor of U.S. aid, which ended that year. Indeed, by 1978, Taiwan's export surplus amounted to more than six percent of its entire GNP! The main catalyst for this explosion in exports was the arrival of massive amounts of foreign investment by OEMs. U.S. and European brands were discovering a new fangled approach to selling their products worldwide at affordable prices—Make it in Taiwan. This led to an astounding boom in the island's industrial capacity, and it was partly encouraged by another round of astute economic policies designed to promote trade and exports.

The Statute for Encouragement of Investment in 1964 laid the groundwork for the coming boom in direct foreign investment. It included a whole string of tax and other export loan incentives that put Taiwan on the cutting edge of economic development and its promotion. Meanwhile, the Government also made sure protectionism was gradually reduced, mainly as a means of showing the world that it was serious about turning Taiwan into a major player in world trade. Along the way, it implemented other critical policies including those that supported labor-intensive industries and creation of jobs for unskilled workers.

Everything seemed to be going Taiwan's way. The Government was exhibiting an unprecedented "golden touch" when it came to economic policies. By 1978, Taiwan had become the world's 21st largest trading nation, and it was the ninth largest trade partner of the U.S. Ten years later, it would be the sixth largest trade nation! Exports rose to 50% of GNP, with imports at 49%, making it perfectly obvious that trade was the lifeblood of the island's economy. Not just the golden goose, but it's very lifeblood.

But there was one other leading factor for growth as well. During this time, the Government also increased investment in the state-owned enterprises, particularly steel, electricity, shipbuilding, tobacco and alcohol, and sugar. These enterprises were able to maintain pace with the rapid development of the private sector, rather than being a drag on the economy as is often the case with such state-owned companies in the typical developing country.

With exports leading the way, Taiwan industrial growth jumped to 11% per year in the Seventies. Those levels were unmatched in the developing world. And, as fate would have it, much of the growth was spurred by tens of thousands of small to medium enterprises, rather than the behemoths typical of Japan. This ants versus elephants model created incredible, broad-based wealth on Taiwan. One fact stands out as a conclusion to this section of exports. Today, nearly one out of every six Taiwan households has someone who owns a home in the United States! Made in Taiwan came to be a butt of international jokes about everything being made on the island, to be sure. But one thing that always amazed me was that even the maker of the most innocuous item, say shoe laces, became a millionaire based on volume. Profit margins were always razor thin, but when you make hundreds of millions of an item each year—guess what? Someone gets rich. And ends up with a house in Los Angeles, four BMWs, and kids at Harvard. Or, if they are even luckier, at Dartmouth!

THE FINAL ACT: INFRASTRUCTURE SPENDING, TECH AND CAPITAL INTENSIVE INDUSTRY

By the end of the Seventies, Taiwan had reached the Turning Point in economics where its per capita GNP was around $10,000. The island had reached First World status at breakneck speed and with one of the most equitable distributions of wealth ever recorded.

As usual, however, the Nationalist Government did not sit still or rest on those laurels. There was still much nation-building work to be done if Taiwan were to be seen as a complete model for Mainland China. The critical remaining area was infrastructural development.

Remember that story about Premier Yu Kuo-hwa and the Chinese penchant for frugality, even when rich? Well, that held up until the late Seventies. But the island's tremendous growth had created a myriad of pressure points on its infrastructure and ability to handle further economic growth (what a problem to have!).

In 1978, then President Chiang Ching-kuo announced a major set of public spending plans for infrastructure projects. These included such things as an interstate highway linking the island from north to south, a new international airport, new ports, new dams and even nuclear plants. The plan was simply called the Ten Major Construction Projects. Simple name, massive effect. All were designed to create the energy, communications and transportation infrastructure for the next period of Taiwan's economic growth.

When I first arrived in 1978, some of these projects were well underway. I first arrived at the old Songshan Airport in downtown Taipei, but left the island ten months later at the new airport outside town. And I took the newly opened freeway to get to the airport.

Ironically, Taiwan's political opposition was very vocal in opposing the Ten Projects. They argued that it was pie-in-the-sky, wasteful spending. Today, you won't hear a soul making ridiculous comments like that. Everyone denies having opposed it. Like when 80% of Americans denied voting for Jimmy Carter, two years after his presidency began!

The key issue here is the desirability of public spending, or not. Taiwan held off for many years until it could actually afford to start making such upgrades. But most developing countries have been sucked into the old leftwing platform that says Big Government should be heavily involved in the economy, and that public spending beats private sector economic growth any day. No matter how often that has been proven to be sheer folly, the idea persists, so much so that it is a raging debate in of all places, the United States.

The Nationalists did not conceive and carry out the

Ten Projects as a means to spur further economic growth. Exports were still doing that. Instead, they implemented the bold plan as a means of providing the infrastructure for continued solid growth, still near ten percent at the time. That the projects created thousands of jobs and had many other collateral positives for private sector economic activity is certainly true. But they were just that— collaterals.

All through the Fifties, Sixties and Seventies—the early stages of development on Taiwan—the Government had a real knack for timing on economic policy.

Which is an excellent segue to the next topic, Government policy toward hi-tech and capital-intensive industries after 1980.

I was, at the time these policies were formulated by the Cabinet, already in the employ of the Taiwan Government as a communications advisor. As part of my job, I had to work closely with nearly all ministries and bureaus, and with certain offices in the Executive Yuan, or Cabinet, where the Premier sits.

I remember one episode very clearly when then Premier Sun Yun-suan, a civil engineer by training and recognized as one of the chief architects of Taiwan's early success, told the nation that the island needed to shift quickly toward a reliance on hi-tech and capital-intensive industries. I was at that press conference, and remember well the reaction in the room. It was like John Kennedy telling NASA, via a speech to the American people, that America was going to land on the moon before the end of the decade! There were many dubious looks. It was a tough sell because Taiwan was so entrenched with thousands of traditional product lines, such as Christmas lights, rubber ducks and, well, as the image back then commanded—just about anything else made under the sun, for sale at K-Mart.

But, as before, he had hit the nail on the head, and within a short two or three years the Government's incentive policies in these new industries had created a fledgling, but noticeably robust IT industry.

What came next was yet another "miracle" of Taiwan's development. Within just a few years, Taiwan became the world's largest producer of computer related gear. It commanded control of the parts infrastructure in IT products, and by the late-Eighties was already the leading producer of PCs, albeit under mostly foreign brand names. Even that would soon change, as names like Acer, Mitac, Proton and tens more quickly rose to prominence in the global IT industry with their own brand names.

Taiwan became so successful in the late Eighties and into the Nineties that world leaders began to fear the worst for the IT industry if Taiwan should happen to have a major natural disaster such as an earthquake (it is prone to these) and/or a typhoon (it is prone to these). The island had come to control so much of the components and finished product infrastructure of the IT industry that these fears were certainly justified. Interestingly, there were never any real worries about social unrest or the like, because Taiwan was considered all along to be rock solid in terms of social and political stability.

The island had been buffeted ten years earlier by the sudden break in diplomatic ties with the U.S. (December 1978). I was a student in Taipei on that fateful night of December 15, when word of the sudden cut in ties was announced by U.S. President Jimmy Carter. The Congress had already recessed and most reps were on airplanes home. Carter chose the night hour and a congressional recess to make the announcement, knowing that it would be highly unpopular. His point was to break with Taiwan in order to establish diplomatic relations with Communist China.

Initially, the island took it very badly. The people, who had always shown unparalleled loyalty to America, felt betrayed. Sporadic anti-Carter violence occurred, and we Americans were cautioned to stay indoors for a few days till fevers cooled down.

What turned the tide was an amazing piece of national stewardship by President Chiang Ching-kuo, who remains perhaps the most-beloved figure in the era of Nationalist Taiwan. Chiang went on national TV to urge the people to turn this setback into a positive opportunity to seek self-reliance, to end the decades old reliance on the U.S. for economic and military support. The people responded in spades. A huge outpouring of national spirit manifested itself, and within months Taiwan was back on track. Carter had failed in his amateurish attempt to make the Taiwan issue disappear in U.S.-China relations. Rather than curl up and collapse, and face absorption into Communist China as some of Carter's Soviet-centric foreign policy advisors probably had hoped, Taiwan emerged from the crisis stronger than ever.

The hallmark of Chiang's self-reliance appeal to the people was his utterance of the phrase, "We must continue to seek progress with stability, and stability with progress." This line alone served as the main catalyst for pulling together the people regardless of their political stripes. Taiwan had already achieved enormous economic success by following this rule of thumb first laid down by Dr. Sun. Only stability creates progress, and then what do you know—progress creates stability. It's not a circle, it's a straight upwards line on the graph of national development. Nobody did it better than Taiwan, and everybody has much to learn from the Taiwan Experience.

This book intended from the start to cover only the early economic and political development on Taiwan. And we will stick to that, because the subject here is the treatment of democracy and its role, if any, in the early stages of national development.

But for the record, it is probably worth noting that Taiwan continues to be one of the more robust economies on the world scene. In the post-1980 era, the Government has continued to make many of the right moves that were needed to maintain growth and stability. Global brands have proliferated from the island, and in the mid-Nineties, a good chunk of the island's manufacturing had begun to migrate to the cheaper labor market directly across the Taiwan Strait in Mainland China. This was a wise move, as the larger players kept their corporate HQs on Taiwan along with their design engineering and R&D. The Taiwan economy thus began its final evolution toward a services economy, but one that still has much industry. Many of the ants referred to earlier are still alive and well, due to their flexibility and nimbleness in the marketplace. The manufacturing shift to the Mainland cannot be over stated, and one fact makes it abundantly clear just how large this shift was: Even today, nearly forty percent of all exports from China come from Taiwan owned or joint-owned factories, mainly in southern China. Taiwan has transferred the wealth of its industrialization and global marketing knowledge and experience to the Mainland, and the results of this have been phenomenal for both sides.

Today, lifestyle issues dominate concerns in Taiwan, not so much economic. That, too, is a sign of a country that has the luxury to worry about luxuries.

It is important to back up here and note that Taiwan reached that all-important STAKEHOLDER SOCIETY point of development probably around 1987-88. That was the point at which the Nationalists decided society was stable enough for the long haul to begin implementing full democracy. It had been nurtured at the grassroots level for decades now, and with Taiwan having achieved the formation of a massive middle class and the eradication of poverty, it was clear that the average citizen had an important stake in social stability as a means of maintaining the hard-earned prosperity. This was not just a Government decision, but one that the majority of Taiwanese certainly shared. They had bought into a Social

Compact that put economics first, with an understanding that when the time was ripe (the STAKEHOLDER SOCIETY point), democracy would be delivered and the people would become the true sovereigns, as predicted by Dr. Sun Yat-sen.

Since our narrative here has reached the point where Taiwan earned its place among developed nations and achieved STAKEHOLDER status, it is time to move on to the subject of how democracy evolved on the island. Once again, Taiwan provides us with some of the best examples of how this can and should be done. We have provided the first half of the "economics first" model of development. Now let's turn our attention to the second half, democracy.

8 DEMOCRATIC DEVELOPMENT

During the 1950s, the United States led a Western effort to implement "overnight" democracy in countries as far apart as Latin America and S.E. Asia. According to authors John Copper and George Chen, Vietnam is a particularly useful example of how this policy failed miserably. Democracy was taking a beating, exactly because it was being implemented in a thoughtless manner that cared little for the history of democratic development. This served to discredit the Western model in the eyes of many a developing country, and while democracy remained a force to be reckoned with as far as global trends go, this series of failed implementations were definitely setbacks.

It is against this backdrop that Taiwan set out to implement its own brand of democracy based on the The Principle of Democracy outlined in Dr. Sun Yat-sen's Three Principles of the People. Taiwan was about to prove the value of patience, and the value of proving over time that the next logical step following achievement of the Stakeholder Society is the development of democracy, naturally.

Taiwan itself, like China in general, had no tradition of democracy. It was just as Confucian oriented as its larger brethren on the Mainland. Going back to its earliest modern history, Taiwan was first ruled by the Dutch as a colony. Chinese pirates led by Koxinga overthrew the Dutch and installed his own Chinese form of autocracy. Later, from 1895 to 1937, Taiwan was ruled as a colony by Japan. And, while the Japanese allowed some elected local assemblies to exist (mainly farmer co-ops and the like) after 1935, the island was tightly controlled in ways that served Japanese economic interests first.

Following Dr. Sun's program, the Nationalist Party under Chiang Kai-shek, having fled to Taiwan following the takeover of Mainland China by Mao's Communists, began implementing democracy in tutelage fashion at the grassroots levels in Taiwan. These occurred at the local and provincial levels. Bear in mind that the Nationalists brought the structure of the entire central government with them to Taiwan, but kept the structure of the provincial government as well, creating what appeared to be an overlap of jurisdictions on the surface, but in reality, there were separations built-into this bizarre system. Many considered the duality nothing but a façade to support the Nationalists' assertion that the Republic of China was alive and well on Taiwan.

From 1945, when Taiwan was returned to China at the end of W.W. II, until 1950, Taiwan had experienced a rough go at any kind of rule. The natives felt that the central government on the Mainland had neglected the island, to which there is much truth. Chiang was embroiled in a civil war with the Communists and had little time to consider problems on the more remote province of Taiwan. Civil unrest ensued, and Chiang's appointed caretaker of Taiwan, General Chen Yi, ruthlessly suppressed public outcries. On February 28, 1947, Chen ordered a bloody crackdown on Taiwanese protesters that killed hundreds. This has become known as 2-2-8, and remains a symbol of some political discontent even today on Taiwan.

When Chiang himself was forced to flee to Taiwan, he quickly took measures to address Chen's excesses. Chen was tried and executed for his crimes against the people in 1951. It was a major move, along with the implementation of Land Reform and grassroots democracy, to assuage Taiwanese discontent with "Mainlander" rule on the island.

There were other pressures that contributed to the Nationalists' need for democratic measures on Taiwan. Chief among these was their need to be accepted by the international community, to have as many nations as possible continue to recognize the de facto and in some cases de jure existence of the Republic of China and its central government. Chiang was surrounded by advisors who understand the PR value of this. On top of this, the United States itself was playing a key role by insisting that the ROC Government make good on its promise (Sun's) to implement democracy sooner than later. Finally, the Nationalists themselves had plenty of incentive to move on democracy as they wanted Taiwan to set an example for all of China. This mindset continued for decades as the

Taiwan experience unfolded.

One of the keys to implementing democracy at any level on Taiwan was the fact that the Nationalists had brought the Constitution of the Republic of China to Taiwan, which formed the basis not only for protecting rights and so forth, but also for setting the stage for democracy. The ROC Constitution was promulgated in 1948, when the elected organs of the ROC Government were still operating on the Mainland. It effectively mirrors many of the rights and provisions found, in say, the U.S. Constitution, but with a sprinkling of inputs from Dr. Sun's Three Principles. This included a pentacameral structure of government (unlike the U.S.'s three branches of government) that added two distinctly Chinese bodies, the Examination Yuan (Government civil servant testing) and the Control Yuan (Government watchdog), both of which have their roots in the Confucian tradition of bureaucracy.

This Constitutional structure did, however, have a central flaw. It kept the national structure for representation, even though the Nationalists now only effectively controlled Taiwan and some smaller outer lying islands belonging to historic and geographic China. This structure caused Taiwan to be the object of ridicule not only at home but also abroad. Representatives from each province of China (36) were kept in their seats in both elected bodies—the Legislative Yuan, and the National Assembly, which addressed not only Constitutional issues but also served as the electoral college for the president and vice president. This structure would be at the heart of Taiwanese political discontent for decades, because the longer those elected on the Mainland served (for life), the more the system became untenable due to issues of aging and so forth. Into the Eighties, the National Assembly in particular became the butt of jokes, with many referring to it as the "wheelchair assembly." Many members were into their nineties, and though they showed up at meetings, they were often seen dozing off. But given the tenuous security situation in 1950 Taiwan, this odd structure did not keep the vast majority of Taiwanese from buying into the Social Compact that was offered to them in 1950.

To reiterate the pertinent elements of that compact, Chiang Kai-shek told the locals that if they sacrificed certain political and civil rights, and allowed the Government to have extra powers during a period of perilous security for the island, and during the democratic tutelage period, then the Government would deliver economic prosperity to the people in exchange for their patience on full political participation. As it relates to democracy, Chiang promised to keep his hands off the local democratization process, so long as the people left matters of the central government to him and the Nationalists and their "national" security apparati.

Also inherent in this compact was the promise that democratic values would be taught in all levels of schools, making it clear that the Nationalists were indeed committed to it, seeing that one could not reasonably expect NOT to deliver democracy if it is being inculcated in the minds of children in the schools. This was taken right out of Dr. Sun's tutelage playbook.

Another critical element of the Social Compact was the Temporary Provisions law that trumped the Constitution on matters of national security and representative government. The Temporary Provisions during the Period of Communist Rebellion were controversial to say the least, as they basically suspended critical parts of the Constitution to provide emergency powers to the president. Under the Provisions, the ROC Government declared martial law on Taiwan, but in an odd twist, they never really implemented anything remotely resembling military rule. Civilian rule was maintained under the façade of martial law, probably for the simple reason of public relations. Taiwan wanted the world, especially the Chinese Communists, to think that Taiwan had martial law as a means of deterring any actions against the island. It was bizarre, but the truth is that it worked.

The Temporary Provisions also featured a ban on new political parties, keeping the tri-party system in tact. The Nationalist Party would remain dominant, even though two other parties were allowed to exist (The Young China Party and the China Democratic Socialist Party). These would, however, be mainly loyal to the ruling party, and have little true independence.

For the Nationalists, the issue was never WILL we implement but WHEN. Their entire government system, the Social Compact and the education system were all geared toward bringing democracy to bear at the right time, after an indefinite period of grassroots tutelage.

In addition, the ROC Constitution in the first place

contained some rather ironic advances over Western models. It had quotas for minority ethnic groups, women and unions in the two nationally elective bodies. It even held spots for overseas Chinese representatives. Again, this was taken from Dr. Sun's playbook of creating a more just, equality-based structure for the nation's political development.

Overall, the stage was set for Taiwan to have authoritarian rule on top with the makings of democracy slowly evolving from below. The Nationalists would have democracy in spirit and partially in structure, but would not operate democratically in reality until years later. As planned. It would be 1980 when a watershed national election would be held to mark the island's transition to full democracy. That election gave rise to full-blown multi-party politics and elections, with no turning back.

THE FIFTIES AND SIXTIES

During the tutelage phase, democracy was implemented at the grassroots level. Though it was dominated by the ruling Nationalist Party, independents were permitted to participate. Local villages, counties and up to the provincial level were all included in the experimentation with democracy.

Observers never found much wrong with these elections. They were largely conducted freely and fairly in the context of the "dome" provided by the national structure on the island.

Land Reform certainly boosted grassroots democracy by providing a timely shot in the arm for the Social Compact (meaning, the Government had already begun to deliver on its prosperity promise as early as 1950-51). As Dr. Sun had noted decades earlier, the key to democracy is stability, and vice versa. Economic progress would provide the much needed stability, which in turn would create conditions needed for successful implementation of democracy.

An interesting outgrowth of the local elections in the early Fifties was the sudden explosion of budgets for local governments. Having given the people a voice, the central government had no choice but to accede to demands for more focus on local development. Already the bottom up effect of grassroots democracy was having a positive effect on society as a whole.

As Copper and Chen conclude in their review of the evolution of elections and democracy on Taiwan, local elections on the island developed without few hitches during the Fifties and into the Sixties. And because the elections often involved unions and other co-op entities, such as farmers' associations, there was a tremendous strengthening of the roots being planted for democracy's later blossoming. I do not see a need to go into the detailed mechanics of Taiwan's grassroots democracy; rather, it is suffice to say that the tutelage period worked as planned, and as we have seen earlier, the island's world-leading economic growth provided the cover needed for a stable environment for democracy to take root. Democracy was now set to take off.

This is not to say, however, that Taiwan had become free of peripheral voices calling for self-determination and an end to martial law, the Temporary Provisions and a return to full constitutional rule. Although a minority, they remained vocal, if not popular. The small percentage of Taiwanese pushing for immediate, radical change would always remain on the stage, despite getting shouted down by the majority in election after election. Indeed, the stable nature of elections at the grassroots level confirmed the validity of the government's blueprint for Taiwan, just as Dr. Sun had predicted.

1969 INTO THE SEVENTIES

As time went on, the United States continued to apply pressure to democratize sooner than later on its Nationalist ally on Taiwan. The Left in the U.S. and Europe considered allies in Taiwan and South Korea to be "embarrassing" to them so long as they paid lip service to democracy but remained authoritarian. These are the same folks who lent moral support to Mao and the Communist regime on Mainland China, which by any measure, was among the most brutal dictatorships on the planet, especially from 1966 to 1976 when the Great Cultural Revolution was raging on the Mainland. Western media criticized Taiwan and South Korea more often than Communist China, despite the fact that the former two had already created record-breaking economic development and were well on their ways to becoming democracies. This hypocrisy on the part of left wing Western media provided much of the impetus for this writer to "get involved" and eventually write this book to set the record straight on democracy's role in national development.

In 1969, the Nationalists responded to pressures both at home and from the U.S. and held supplementary elections (adding new seats, not contesting existing seats) to begin addressing the oddity of the national (all China) representative nature of the National Assembly and Legislative Yuan. It featured an expansion of the number of Taiwan seats in each body (11 added to Legislature, 15 to National Assembly). While many saw this as window dressing, it did set the stage for further elections along the same lines, gradually leading to normalization of the representation of these bodies, meaning Taiwanization of them.

In 1972, the pace of liberalization and reform began to pick up, this after the appointment of Chiang Ching-kuo as the nation's premier. A son of Chiang Kai-shek, this Chiang would prove to be one of the most effective and beloved leaders in world history.

The younger Chiang made it his mission to bring more Taiwanese into the political process and into central government service (with few exceptions, until now Taiwanese had been relegated mostly to local and provincial roles). He also would usher in a new era of freedoms for oppositionists who were starting to form a block that would become known as the "dang wai," or "outside the Party" (KMT).

Chiang Kai-shek died on April 5, 1975, and in the

island's first peaceful transfer of presidential power, though in the context of one-Party rule, his vice president, Yen Chia-kang took over. Yen would serve for about a year before the National Assembly would hold presidential elections and elect Chiang Ching-kuo president. Although the ROC Constitution provides that the president is more a figure head of state and the premier is tasked with running the day-to-day affairs of central Government, the Nationalists retained the model in effect during the Temporary Provisions that placed real power in the hands of the presidency.

That said, President Chiang immediately began to show his commitment to fulfilling his father's social compact. One of his first moves was to appoint Sun Yun-suan (no relation to Dr. Sun), an engineer by trade, as the nation's premier. He instructed Sun to come up with the plans that would maintain Taiwan's amazing pace of economic development. Sun had been instrumental in the early years of Land Reform and infrastructural development.

Chiang also increased the pace of so-called Taiwanization in the central government. He strengthened the technocracy by bringing aboard mostly U.S. educated economists, bankers, engineers and scholars into the Cabinet. By 1978, Taiwan's Cabinet was the most educated on the planet, with nearly all ministers and vice-ministers holding Ph.Ds. Along the way, Chiang cracked down on cronyism within the Party and government, which also helped strengthen the development of the technocracy.

At about the time Chiang became Premier in 1972, Taiwan was also starting to feel the heat of the impact of the emerging relations between the U.S. and Communist China. Secretary of State Henry Kissinger's trips to Beijing in 1971 and 1972 put the writing on the wall clearly for the Nationalists on Taiwan, and pressures built to gain international acceptance for their exiled regime on Taiwan. The ROC on Taiwan was in the fight for its life in justifying its nationhood status in the eyes of the international community, as opposed to falling into the trap of being seen exclusively as a "renegade" province of China, as Beijing continued to hold. If anything, Chiang Ching-kuo had an amazing knack for capturing the timing for needed reforms, while still moving in the calculated fashion required to maintain stability on Taiwan. The balancing act was exacerbated by opposing forces on Taiwan itself, with localization of politics competing with that at the national level. With virtual Mainlander control at the national level and Taiwanese control at the local levels (provincial on down), Chiang needed to make moves to keep the island's political development on track.

Also problematic at the time was the issue of the Nationalists' stated goal of someday returning to the Mainland. With U.S.-Communist China détente in full-swing, that goal began to sound more like a myth, which could eventually undermine Nationalist rule on Taiwan, if left unaddressed. The breakthrough in Washington-Beijing relations was certainly a diplomatic setback for Taipei, and it gave rise to a new level of student activism on Taiwan, mainly with regard to self-determination and representative issues.

On top of that, social and economic change had created pressure on democratization. As we have argued all along here, democracy evolves naturally out of economic prosperity, and especially after the Stakeholder Society milestone has been reached (around 1978 in Taiwan's case). Political participation is the next logical step in the process, and on Taiwan, that meant a process compounded with the existence of the simultaneous need for Taiwanization.

Simply put, Chiang was under much pressure to further liberalize but without upsetting the apple cart of stability, which would doom the island's robust economics. And he delivered by boldly holding a series of supplemental elections to greatly increase the participation of Taiwanese in the nation's nationally elected bodies. Elections were held in 1972 when he was premier, and again in 1975, adding tens of new members representing areas in Taiwan.

Meanwhile, the KMT had itself become a majority Taiwanese Party by this time, and Chiang saw to it that this trend continued within the Party, and not just the central government. By 1978, 87% of those serving in the Legislative Yuan were Taiwanese. The National Assembly still had a ways to go toward a Taiwan majority.

In 1977, Chiang responded to all the mounting pressures by holding major local elections that would be the first to feature full-blown (real) opposition to KMT rule. The oppositionists smartly played by the rules of not pushing forbidden themes such as independence, but they did begin pushing harder for a faster pace of Taiwanization and political reforms and liberalizations.

Chiang's sense of timing, Taiwanization policies and his genuine commitment to nurturing political competition continued into the Eighties. But not without a rocky phase out of the Seventies.

In December 1978, the U.S. suddenly and unannounced broke relations with Taipei. That was followed by a complete lack of U.S. representation on the island until May 1979 when the Taiwan Relations Act (TRA) kicked in and established an informal U.S. presence on the island. To counter the de-recognition policy of President Jimmy Carter, the U.S. Congress established the TRA to help maintain stability on Taiwan and create conditions for Taiwan to remain as a strong ally of the U.S.

Despite these setbacks, President Chiang implemented a summer-long series of reforms that opened up press freedoms, leading to more activism and more calls for quicker reforms and liberalizations.

Unfortunately, the progress was set back by a Human Rights Day riot that broke out in the southern city of Kaohsiung, Taiwan's second largest city. Led by "dang wai" radicals who were part of a group involved with FORMOSA MAGAZINE, a large group of protesters attacked police lines, which had been told not to fight back. The ensuing chaos left tens of police badly injured, but few rioters. It was the worst case of violence since the 2-2-8 incident in 1947, and created shock waves throughout the country. This event, later known as the Kaohsiung Incident, proved a turning point, but not as you might expect. The vast majority of the public turned against the oppositionist movement, arguing that it was in no one's interest to bring such instability to the island, especially at a time when so many other destabilizing factors, mainly from abroad, were all around. Sound familiar? It was a major confirmation of the success of the Social Compact, with the majority of citizens still firmly committed to it.

Following the Incident, in early 1980 progressive legislators began to pass laws aimed at further liberalizations. A major compromise was reached, and was embodied in the breakthrough Public Officials Election & Recall Law of 1980. This law completely revamped the system and for all intents and purposes, began the process of dismantling the Temporary Provisions. It was widely seen as a vast improvement over the Provisions, and included such major reforms as legitimizing the dang wai, and according all new rights to them and other oppositionists. It paved the way for the island's first major electoral test on the national level—the December 1980 election. Unlike previous national elections on Taiwan, it would be the first non-supplemental one, in other words a real general election with existing seats up for grabs.

John Copper has called this a "watershed" event in Taiwan's democratization. Not only would it be a major test for stability, but it would also give rise to an all new era of rapid liberalizations, leading to full democracy within a few short years.

For its part, the KMT campaigned on a platform that highlighted its delivery of its side of the bargain of the

Social Compact. Economic prosperity was enjoyed by most people, the island's stability had maintained and democracy was being nurtured in a stable, progressive fashion. As planned. For its part, the now more organized Dang Wai ran on a platform pushing for speedier reforms and liberalizations, particularly in the areas of civil rights and social justice. Specifically, the Dang Wai posited a platform that included nine issues: 1) more seats for Taiwanese in nationally elected bodies; 2) elections for Taiwan Governor and major city mayors; 3) even more appointments of Taiwanese in high levels of government; 4) greater freedoms of speech and press; 5) fewer campaign restrictions; 6) abolishment of the Temporary Provisions; 7) review of political trials; 8) relinquishing of KMT powers, and 9) freedom to form new parties.

The election did proceed under some "gentlemen's agreements." These included bi-partisan agreements barring support for communism, Taiwan independence from historic and geographic China and for negotiations with Communist China. As part of the tutelage period, restrictions on the official campaign period were observed (ten days) as were restrictions on signage, noise, etc.

Still, the election was highlighted by "entertaining" vitriol, which caught the public's attention and made it almost a fun process to witness and participate in. Foreign observers noted that the process had few irregularities of import, and that overall it was fair, open and clean. It saw 66% voter turnout (election days on Taiwan are holidays, thus encouraging political participation. That's something the U.S. can learn from Taiwan, given that U.S. voter turnout ranges in the forties).

The results gave both sides reasons to claim victory. Although the KMT won 63 out of 76 seats up for election in the National Assembly, and 56 of 70 in the Legislative Yuan, and eighty percent of the vote overall, the Dang Wai still saw their progress as a major step forward. The problem with that position is that the KMT could also take credit for that progress, being as it was the steward of the entire process. Certainly President Chiang was pleased, as his agenda was moving forward on both accounts.

The 1980 election also featured some other interesting tidbits. Most of the winners from either the KMT or Dang Wai were Taiwanese. Women also made a good showing, winning nearly 15% of seats. Business persons took most seats, with many stubborn ideologues on both sides losing out to these more conservative voices for stability. Those with higher educations fared better on the whole. Finally, and perhaps somewhat ironically, the largest single vote getter was a member of the more vocal oppositionists. As a block, the Dang Wai clearly saw that its role as a genuine opposition "party" was beginning to take shape. In the end, an "informed and highly enlightened" public was pleased with the process and the result.

The KMT saw the election as having validated its brand of "non-martial" martial law, and there was much celebrating over having made a major step forward in implementing Dr. Sun's Three Principles of the People. The economy first principle, which had guided Taiwan's spectacular development to the present, surely received the most important stamp of approval. But most importantly, perhaps, was the reaffirmation of President Chiang's long held axiom that Taiwan needed "stability to create progress, progress to create stability."

THE NEXT STEPS

A year later, a provincial election showed similar results with sustained progress and stability. By now, provincial elections had begun to mirror national ones in tone and import. Local elections held in 1982 also took on the flavor of national referendums on important issues of the day. And, perhaps more importantly, the Dang Wai began to function more like a bonafide political party, if not in name.

But the Nationalists or KMT were becoming increasingly uneasy about losing control of the process at the national level. Locally, some of that had already begun to occur in the south with increasing gains among Dang Wai candidates. They feared a similar trend would take hold on the national level, making it harder to guide the process through to a more mature end result.

In 1981, the case of Chen Wen-cheng, a Taiwanese professor at Carnegie-Mellon in the USA, brought tensions to a head. Chen was found murdered after being in police custody. The government says it released him unharmed and that someone else was responsible for his death. Chen was a vocal opponent of the KMT. His murder remains a mystery today, with pro-government supporters saying the radical opposition had him killed for "ratting" on them, while the opposition still maintains that he was tortured and killed. From my perch within the Government Information Office, where I had access to police reports and other crucial evidence, I always thought it was most likely his pals got rid of him thinking he had become a snitch. The government had no motive to kill such a man, knowing the damage it would do to its representation. But the radicals knew who would get the blame either way. Hmmm?

The local elections later in the year proved to be more unruly and a bit crazy, with nutty campaign antics starting to come out of the woodwork. Some of the candidates bit the heads off live chickens to demonstrate their loyalty to a cause (it's a Chinese thing!). Bribery, vote-buying (often times with rice, soap and other household goods) and other chicanery also reared their ugly heads. This would further contribute to the KMT's unease about the direction the nation's democracy was taking.

But cooler heads still prevailed on both sides. Most everyone began to chalk up these irregularities to fads or as signs of immaturity in the democratic process. Still, vote-buying would have to be addressed, or better yet, nipped in the bud.

Voter turnout for these raucous elections was an astounding 70%, with both sides again claiming victory, despite the KMT once again winning 80% of the seats. Higher education continued to be a strong factor for candidates on both sides, and women made more progress in numbers. For the first time, however, many of those elected to office were younger than the demographic prominent in previous elections. The Dang Wai asserted it had made new inroads all around, while the KMT stuck to its guns on progress and stability, and delivering on long-standing promises.

Although the KMT clearly could claim victory in terms of the numbers, President Chiang nevertheless took more action to strengthen the Party's hand. Shortly after the election, he reshuffled the Cabinet. Importantly, he made Taipei Mayor Lee Teng-hui the new Governor of Taiwan, perhaps the most important post held by a Taiwanese thus far.

In the 1982 County elections, the KMT won 682 of 799 seats, with all previous election trends continuing with few problems. This would remain the case throughout the Chiang era. In the run up to a 1983 supplementary Legislative Yuan election on the national level, President Chiang guided a new election law through to its fruition in the Legislature. This new law extended the campaign period to six weeks and offered the opposition more leeway than ever before. It also set the pattern for future development and defined all the rules more clearly than ever before, setting the stage for complete democratization at the national level. The 1983 election marked the first time that the KMT began to identify itself separately from the Government (a much needed trend, as the overlap of Party and Government was quickly becoming archaic in the context of the new political realities on Taiwan). For its part, the Dang Wai actually began to split into two factions: A radical arm still bent on Taiwan independence from historic China, and a more moderate faction that was still content campaigning on such issues as civil rights and full constitutional rule. The election saw a lower 63% turnout, with the KMT winning 62 of 71 seats. The Dang Wai captured six seats, of which four were from the more radical faction. 73% of the popular vote went to the KMT. Eight seats went to women, 66 to Taiwanese. 53 seats were won by persons under the age of 40. The young and highly educated continued their dominance, especially from the business sector. The more vociferous stance of the radicals may have helped attract many votes to their small number of candidates, but overall their performance was viewed as a setback for the Dang Wai movement as a whole. The radicalism was still seen overall as a potentially destabilizing factor, still not supported by a vast majority of Taiwanese. Stability remained THE core concern of that vast majority of citizens, and the Dang Wai began to struggle with its identity as a protest party versus a bonafide opposition party.

In 1987, President Chiang decided to give them a helping hand out of that quagmire by introducing a major advance: He decided the time was ripe to allow the Dang Wai to form into a formal political party. The basis for this breakthrough was his belief that the KMT and Dang Wai had evolved peaceably into competitors and not enemies. He saw a healthy ruling-opposition party system emerging, as planned. From then on, the Dang Wai would become known as the Democratic Progressive Party, or DPP for short. It was actually another timely, brilliant stroke, this time aimed at encouraging the opposition to close ranks around more moderate policies.

President Chiang died in 1988. He is widely viewed as the architect of modern Taiwan, both economically and politically speaking. It was a shock to the nation, but his record of achievement would prove to serve him well in death. His successor, former Governor Lee Teng-hui, who had been elected as Vice President a year and a half prior, became the first Taiwanese to serve as ROC President. And thus, with his death, Chiang marked the final transition to full Taiwanization and peaceful democratic development. Although his stewardship would be sorely missed, it was also true that he left behind lasting institutions that were well-equipped to carry the torch of Dr. Sun's Three Principles forward. A robust, at times rowdy democracy had grown out of the spectacular economic miracle that was achieved on Taiwan, and it had done so without a bloody revolution and the inherent instability that had marked so many democratic movements around the world to date.

In 2000, the island held its first general elections for president (and not via the National Assembly electoral college). As a novelty, the DPP candidate, Chen Shui-bian, won but only after the KMT had split in two with Lien Chan running as the Party man and James Soong, the breakaway candidate, running separately. Together they won 58 percent of the vote to Chen's 36. Nevertheless, the Taiwan voters seemed ready to try something different than the old and tested KMT, and the DPP finally got its shot at power.

But moving from "loyal" opposition to ruling party proved difficult for the relatively inexperienced DPP. They knew little about economics, and were only geared for playing incessant politics. During Chen's first four-year term, he flirted with the idea of independence a bit too often, and Taiwan's standing in the world was ill-affected as a result. The more Chen talked about independence, the less respected Taiwan became, largely because independence was seen for what it is—a destabilizing factor not only across the Taiwan Strait to Mainland China but in East Asia in general. All world powers including the U.S. have come down firmly against the proposition, yet Chen continued to play with fire. Meanwhile, the DPP's lack of experience as stewards of an economy proved detrimental to the island's economic well-being, and the economy began to slow at levels never seen before.

The 2004 election provided a referendum on Chen's presidency and DPP rule in general. Behind by two or more points in the polls with one day to go, and running against a KMT team of Lien and Soong (a coalition arrangement), Chen was "saved" by a mysterious assassination attempt the night before the election. This "event" proved helpful to Chen's cause, prompting the DPP faithful to swarm to the polls. While many observers on Taiwan and abroad view the attempt on Chen's life as a staged event, he nevertheless won by a slim margin.

Too bad for Taiwan. Chen's second term would be marked by corruption not seen in Asia since the days of Marcos in The Philippines. The economy would continue its downward spiral, and eventually, Chen would fall as far from grace as possible by landing in prison for life after being convicted of emptying public coffers into his private bank accounts around the world. Ostensibly to help fund Taiwan independence cells around the globe. Doesn't matter why. The damage to Taiwan was incalculable as some started to see the island as just another banana republic.

But, that later proved not to be the case. In the 2008 presidential election, the KMT candidate Ma Ying-jeou, a youngish, Harvard educated lawyer, won easily and immediately set out to restore Taiwan's credibility among the ranks of democracies. His efforts were confirmed with his re-election in 2012 by an even wider margin. Ma has made co-existence and cooperation with Mainland China one of the hallmarks of his platform, and to much avail, as Taiwanese businesses have also made the migration to investing and operating on the Mainland. Now, not only do Taiwanese have a stakeholder share in stability on Taiwan itself, but in their relations with Mainland China as well. This bodes well for cross-Strait progress and prosperity. The issue of reunification of Taiwan and the Mainland is not seen by either side as a priority, for now. Leave it to the Chinese on both sides to put economics first!

Today, Taiwan remains one of the most robust democracies on the planet. For the purposes of this book, we do not cover the period since full democratization took place, because our intent here is to argue the case for democracy's role in the early stages of national development. It was important, however, to cover some of the highlights following the Eighties since we need to make the point that Taiwan remains a robust democracy.

9 CHINA: FAST ON THE HEELS OF TAIWAN

If any country is misunderstood by foreigners, it is China. Having thrown off the shackles of Communism and Maoism some thirty years ago, China has developed economically in nothing short of spectacular fashion.

Left in the trail of breakneck development, however, is one of the most contradictory nations in history. Indeed, China is dominated by its contradictions, which then form the leading cause for it being so widely misunderstood around the world. Is China rich? Is it poor? Is it developed? Is it developing? Is it civilized? Or is it still backward? Is it stable or is it in a constant state of chaos? Is it friend or foe of the West?

These and so many other questions point to a country of vast contradictions. Even the tourist to China can see the manifestations of these contradictions in plain view. I am most moved by the contradiction offered by the 2008 Olympic Opening Ceremony in Beijing. That was July. A worldwide TV viewing audience of hundreds of millions of people was stunned by the fabulous display of modern architecture throughout the Olympic premises, and by the state-of-the-art technologies used in the ceremony itself. Yet, a short few months later, some of the same worldwide TV audience was horrified by the scenes of the Sichuan earthquake that crumbled large portions of the more underdeveloped western parts of China. Scenes showed adobe-made elementary schools collapsed, with hundreds of children killed under the rubble. The scenes evoked common Third World imagery, and clashed greatly with what had been seen months prior in Beijing. Many asked: Is this the same country?

That pretty much sums up China's current state. It is all of the above. It is neither here nor there in terms of being rich or poor, developed or underdeveloped, and so on. It is also neither here nor there in terms of being either a command economy and/or a free market economy. China is caught in between worlds, and thus it becomes easily misunderstood.

To understand China, one has to go back to the beginning of Communist rule in the country in 1949. The whole of the Maoist era needs to be understood before one can fully grasp how far China has really come since that era ended. And where it's going today. I argue that China is finally on the right path of development, even though it faces HUGE problems and obstacles along the way.

It turns out that I am one of a handful of foreigners who experienced China before the end of the Maoist era. As a student at Peking University in Spring of 1980, I caught the tail end of the era. Deng Xiaoping, who would emerge as the transformational, post-Communism leader, was just beginning to openly talk about reforms and liberalizations. Nothing had been implemented yet. The country was still covered in Maoist propaganda, with massive billboards propagating the coming victory of communism over capitalism, and urging workers of the world to unite to defeat capitalism. Not a Coca Cola or Nike billboard in sight!

It was only a short four years after the end of one of history's worst man-made disasters, the Great Cultural Revolution, so the nation was still mostly exhausted and more importantly, still fearful of its own Government. Citizens still feared other citizens; neighbors still feared neighbors, and the fear even penetrated the family unit. Young Chinese today, upon hearing that I lived in the "Old China," invariably ask me what it was like. Many of them have heard stories from their parents and grandparents and aunts and uncles, but they also yearn to hear a foreigner's take. And since there were so few of us around back in that day, I guess one could understand why they might consider it a rare opportunity to hear such a view. In any case, I always tell them the same thing: Just think of today's North Korea (in Chinese they call it Chao Xian) and you can have a vision of what China was like in 1980 and before. They get it. And it worries them. From everything they know about North Korea, and from everything they have heard from parents and grand parents, aunts and uncles and so on, and now from this foreign devil, it makes sense to them that the past was bad, like *really* bad, and that it is not a desirable thing at all to return to. Amen to that.

And most even agree that North Korea is an embarrassment for China (who props it up politically and economically as a fellow "communist state" to this day) stuck as it is in a perpetual state of totalitarianism of the worst kind. One cannot understand today's China without first understanding its ugly Maoist past.

So, let's do a rather extensive overview of the Old China, first.

The Old China: The Lost Decades

When Mao Zedong and the Chinese Communist Party (CCP) came to power on October 1, 1949, after a long grueling civil war with Chiang Kai-shek and the Nationalist Party (KMT), he declared that "China had stood up." He was referencing China's long tradition of suffering at the hands of foreign imperialism, unequal treaties, and the like. He was saying those days were over. And that notion alone was cause for the Chinese masses to throw their support behind the new regime, which otherwise, had gained power through violent revolution and as Mao himself always liked to say, "through the barrel of a gun." But Mao successfully played the nationalism card as well.

Throughout the Communist revolution Mao had made promises bordering on social compacts. A mostly underclass, agrarian revolution, Mao promised to free the country from the shackles of foreign imperialism, poverty and disease. He held out the Soviet vision of a new egalitarian society in which the workers ruled, and which would gradually cleanse itself of all vestiges of decadent capitalism and bourgeois influences. That message must have seemed appealing to the five hundred million Chinese who were dirt poor at the time. In fact, when Mao took power China was listed as the third poorest nation on earth.

Unfortunately for the Chinese people, and nation, what came next was nothing short of a totally lost thirty year period. Soon after taking power, Mao then used power to crush any and all opposition to his rule, and Communist Party rule. Millions were persecuted and killed, especially anyone with close ties to the former KMT Government. His idea of achieving unity was to eliminate anyone opposed to you. He succeeded in a short one or two years.

But his rule also began to take on a cult of personality that would some day reach unparalleled heights in human history. By the mid 1950s, government was taking a back seat to the "Thought of Mao Zedong." Anyone who dared challenge Mao was eliminated, either by exile to the countryside to grow carrots or by death.

Orwell's Animal Farm had come to fruition in China. Promising during the revolution to deliver the masses from the evils of the past, Mao had now become the top Pig, ruling over the other farm animals with an iron fist. Economically, he was hell bent on creating his version of a just society in which everyone would be equally poor and, as it turned out, equally enslaved. To this day the Communist Party inculcates the masses with the phrase "jie fang hou," which means "after liberation," referring to the period after Mao took power, up till today. Really? That in itself is a bold Orwellian lie. Rather than liberate the Chinese, Mao proceeded to enslave them in the Animal Farm.

That's the political and economic reality of the time. What's worse is that Mao also set out to totally destroy nearly all vestiges of China's great, millennia old culture. His vision of the proletarian state offered that it was necessary not only to create a new state, but also to create a new man, with a new culture. That would be a tall task for anyone as the Chinese are probably the most cultural-centric people on the planet, and without doubt the proudest of their long cultural tradition. Using the barrel of the gun again, Mao set out to completely rid China of its former identity with the stated lofty goal of creating a new society, a Soviet state. This effort would come to a head later on in the Great Cultural Revolution. We'll cover that in more detail in a few moments.

But first, it is necessary to cover Mao's near apocalyptic economic policies that began with the Great Leap Forward in 1958-62. Having claimed to have had a brilliant vision enter his mind (as nearly all Communist Dear Leaders do), Mao proclaimed that it was time for the country to make a giant leap toward Communism, toward the utopian state. And for that to happen, the country would have to greatly multiply its industrial and agricultural production, surpassing even that of his Soviet mentors. And he planned to do it in a short five years.

What ensued was one of the worst man-made disasters in history. The Great Leap, which essentially meant speeding up communization of the means of industrial and agricultural production, led to an unprecedented era of mass starvation throughout China. Today, scholars tend to agree on the figure of 58 million deaths attributable to the Great Leap Forward.

It was here that Mao got his first lesson on the irrelevance of the imported ideology of Marxism-Communism to China. He also should have learned the lesson that Communism would be an abject failure, anywhere. How does one increase production by disincentivizing the workers to produce? It was insanity at best. And points to the larger picture of Communism's failure overall in the 20th century. It is an inhuman form of economics, premised on creating a new man to make it happen. Leave that to God, Heaven and human genome projects, not to the likes of Mao, Marx and Lenin, was the lesson of the 20th Century. As it was, the Great Leap Forward amounted to one of the largest great leaps backward for any society in human history!

During this time another thread of Mao's rule began to crystallize. Since he was not an economist and had no clue about economics, he opted for his own style of rule that focused on politics and constant revolution, constant social upheaval to rid oneself of the past toward creating a bold new Communist future. This point is important in the aftermath of the Great Leap Forward, and the lessons it SHOULD have brought to Mao and the CCP. But since Mao was already deeply entrenched in his implementation of constant revolution, constant upheaval, rather than learning the obvious from the Great Leap Forward, Mao turned right around and implemented yet another maniacal campaign, this one known as the Let a Hundred Flowers Bloom, a Hundred Thoughts Grow.

The Hundred Flowers campaign was one of the worst traps ever set by a national leader on his own people. Essentially, Mao wanted the intellectual class in China to believe that he was sincere about learning lessons from the Great Leap Forward. So he wanted their inputs on the future direction he and the Party should take.

Yeah, right. Again, what ensued really has no words to describe. Many intellectuals took the bait, and began to openly criticize Mao and the CCP. The flowers began to bloom alright, and the thoughts began to flow, but soon Mao had heard enough, and probably as planned from the start of this most cynical of all campaigns, he quickly began to crack down on them. Thousands were executed, and tens of thousands were sent off to Communist indoctrination camps or banished to farms in the poorest areas of the country. It would be the last time intellectuals in China would ever trust Mao. His bush hog regime cut down every single flower that sprang up under the campaign.

Lesson learned, right? Not. If you think the Great Leap and Hundred Flowers campaigns were bad, you ain't heard nothing yet when it comes to the Great Cultural Revolution of 1966-1975. In my view, this period in Chinese history is among the worst in all of human history. It actually pains me to believe that. As a son-in-law of China, I wish my adopted country did not hold that title.

But, such a claim is easily backed by a simple narrative of the main things that went on during the Revolution. I have some credentials with regard to this campaign, as I edited the English version of a 900-page book produced by historians associated with the KMT Party in Taiwan. It was a complete history of the period, with insights gained from key players who had escaped and made their way either to Taiwan or Hong Kong. I also studied the period extensively in college.

The Cultural Revolution virtually shut down China for ten years. The country was nearly totally cut off from the outside world. Save for Henry Kissinger's secret trips to Beijing in 1971-72, and Nixon's opening and visits to China that followed, coupled with Japan's establishment of diplomatic relations with China in 1972, the outside world was left largely in the dark about what was transpiring in China.

That did not have to be so. During that time, Taiwan and Hong Kong were often citing intelligence reports that followed events in China. Who else could have such good intelligence in China? Yet, the West mostly ignored the information coming out of Taiwan and Hong Kong, calling it "anti-Communist propaganda," and therefor biased and unreliable. That is a real shame. Years later, after he had emerged as China's transformational leader in the late 70s, Deng Xiaoping, when asked about the Cultural Revolution during a press conference on his first visit to the U.S., responded by saying, "Whatever you have heard about it, it was much worse than that. Many times over." Turns out that for all those years Taipei and Hong Kong were in fact not spouting anti-Communist propaganda but rather the facts.

Interesting that a Chinese Communist leader, no matter how liberal, would publicly admit to such a thing! It was only then that the West began to examine the Cultural Revolution through a more realistic prism, one that included distilling the long held views of the likes of Taipei.

The point of the Cultural Revolution was to re-energize the country back to the purist ideology of Maoism. Seems an odd undertaking for a leader who had just conducted two nearly apocalyptic campaigns in his own name. But this would be the REAL deal: An all-out effort to subjugate the entire society to the whims of Mao and his ubiquitous thought. Mao unleashed it, but later on, even he could not believe what he had done. The campaign was executed behind the scenes by what became known later as the Gang of Four, a clique closest to Mao and led by his wife Jiang Qing. Jiang was a fire breathing believer in all things Mao, and the Gang of Four largely took on her persona in bringing the darkest forces imaginable to bear on China's innocent masses.

Ever fearful and distrustful of those around him, Mao chose a millions strong cadre of young Red Guards to implement the Revolution. He knew he could count on their youthful ignorance and fervor to carry out his vision to re-energize the nation toward its goal of achieving pure Communism. They were unleashed upon society to carry out two main goals: Destroy any and all vestiges of the old culture, and seek out and destroy all those who would oppose the Dear Leader, the Chairman. The nightmare that followed was probably unprecedented in human history. The Red Guards, mostly teens and twenty-somethings, were set loose on the country. They pillaged and ransacked China's most sacred cultural relics and national treasures. They played policeman, judge and executor all-in-one in eliminating those even remotely suspected of opposing Mao Thought. What I consider to be the scariest aspect of all this is that people turned on each other as a means of survival. Neighbors reported on neighbors, sometime fabricating accusations of anti-Mao behavior just to prove their own loyalty. Things got so bad that even family members turned on family members, often the young turning against the elders. The nightmare went on for ten long years, with society teetering on total collapse along the way.

It is here that a side story is very demonstrative of how Chinese today view this period in their Communist history. When the War Against Japan was still raging in the early Forties, Chiang Kai-shek took pains to pack up and move China's oldest, most priceless treasures from the National Palace Museum in Beijing. By treasures, we are talking items thousands of years old, and numbering some quarter of a million artifacts. During the War, and during the Chinese civil war with the Communists that followed, Chiang and the Nationalists kept moving the treasures by truck, train and boat from one place to another gradually making their way further and further south to keep them safe. Now, it was no longer the Japanese that posed a threat to the treasures, but the Chinese Communists as well, who were already espousing the Maoist tenant of destroying the past to create a new society. Eventually, the treasures made their way to Taipei when Chiang and about 2 million Mainlanders fled to the island in 1948-49, prior to Mao's takeover of the Mainland.

For decades Mainland Chinese were conditioned to view Chiang as a thief of untold proportions for having "stolen" China's greatest treasures. They called Chiang all kinds of bad names, including robber and thief, when referring to him at all times.

My, my how things have changed now. Today, Chiang is largely viewed as a hero for having saved China's greatest relics from the hateful, destructive paws of Mao's Red Guards! It is a complete reversal when you talk to folks in China today, and understandably so. During the Cultural Revolution, some eighty percent of China's great age old cultural relics were wiped out. Only since Deng Xiaoping did the Communists finally figure out how unpopular that tenant of Maoism was, and how valuable China's cultural tradition could be as a magnate for foreign tourism. Sorry though it is, most of what foreigners see in China today, stuff that is really old, has been discovered and uncovered since 1980. There is a lot left in as yet unopened or undiscovered imperial tombs. But the fact remains that the cream of the crop of China's treasures are still in Taipei, in what Taipei calls the National Palace Museum, widely considered to be one of the top two or three museums in the world. Ironically, the Mainland Chinese view of this has evolved so much that they now have a prevalent joke about it. It goes: Beijing has a

National Palace but no stuff. Taipei has stuff but no National Palace. It's a play on words that also has political meanings when it comes to Taipei's legitimacy.

Today, there is not a single Chinese who actually believes the assault on China's culture was called for. Mao gets the blame, through and through.

Meanwhile, the Cultural Revolution also witnessed another unbelievable assault on one of China's most treasured institutions: Education. Believe it or not, but for ten years schools at every level in China were completely shut down. All that mattered was ardent fury for Mao and his Thought. The CCP and Government no longer trusted teachers and intellectuals. They could not be trusted with Mao's sacred words and campaigns. That would be left to the uneducated masses swarming the country in an orgy of anti-establishment violence. For their part, teachers were sent to the countryside to perform hard labor. They were joined by thousands of Party cadres who were deemed suspect in their adherence to Mao Thought. Among these was none other than Deng Xiaoping himself. Deng spent 11 years in exile, only to make a historic comeback in the years following the Revolution.

Imagine a national leader that shuts down all schools for ten years, for the purpose of "cleansing society" and inculcating the masses with the purity of his own thought? Such a leader is inconceivable in the modern Western tradition, unless you find parallels with Adolph Hitler, which, actually, do exist between him and Mao.

During the Revolution, the CCP itself was not immune

to upheaval and chaos. Mao used the period to eliminate his closest rivals in the Party, save for one, Zhou Enlai, who served as Mao's long time righthand man on foreign affairs. Zhou was Premier of the nation, to Mao's Chairman of the Party, but he existed purely at the whim of Mao.

That is a real shame. For if it was not for Zhou, there would be no China today. China would have totally collapsed into the abyss of chaos and societal breakdown if it were not for Zhou's ability to have at least a part of Mao's ear. In short, Zhou was the angel on Mao's shoulder, constantly nudging him away from his maniacal tendencies. Of course, Zhou was not always effective, hence the national calamities that marked the Maoist era. It is the assertion of this observer, however, that Zhou still deserves credit for holding China together, against tremendous odds. Zhou is given credit widely for handling China's delicate foreign relations, especially the triangular Cold War ties with the former Soviet Union and the USA. As Henry Kissinger often relates throughout his book ON CHINA, Zhou Enlai was indispensable to Mao and China.

Zhou survived all the purges, all the campaigns almost to the very end. Most say that makes him complicit in Mao's maniacal regime. But I share the Kissingerian view that Zhou did what he had to do to survive, and that rather than be seen as an accomplice, he should be regarded as a victim, and should be remembered more as the glue that held China together under the worst of circumstances. Zhou was finally forced out of office with only two years left in his life, in 1974. Mao finally gave in to the whims of the Gang of Four, led by his wife Jiang Qing, and had Zhou removed from the center of power completely. He was rarely seen in public after that, and died in February 1976, some seven months before Mao himself died. Zhou's funeral revealed the extent to which the Chinese people had come to revere him for his clear-headedness and contributions to keeping China from going completely mad at the hands of Mao. Mao was said to be furious over the public outpouring for Zhou, but he was also said to have admitted much earlier on that he knew Zhou had ended up more popular than the Chairman himself. That's for sure.

By 1975, Mao's own failing health contributed to his eventual burnout for the Revolution he had unleashed. The Gang of Four had been exposed and been made the scapegoats, and Mao thus held on to the levers of power ever so tenuously. Before his death, however, he did do something many had thought would not happen: he arranged for a successor. Not a typical action for a ruler who had achieved the greatest heights of unrivaled power, even to the extent of having successfully created one of history's most effective cults of personality. He appointed Hua Guofeng, Party Secretary for Gansu Province, as his eventual, chosen successor. When Mao died in September 1976, Hua was ready to take over the reins of power.

But where was he to go? Was it practical for him to lead a party built on Maoist Thought out of the Maoist Era? Or would he necessarily have to stick with Maoism to survive? On the heels of the Cultural Revolution, the latter path did not seem feasible. The country was totally destroyed and burned out spiritually for any quick return to

Maoist policies. But on the other hand, the CCP had staked its reason for being on Marxism, Maoism and Communism. Hua chose a path of neither here nor there, but more resembling the status quo.

He did not last long. The nation was begging for a different course. There could be no more chances of another national calamity.

The Deng Era Begins

Then came Deng Xiaoping. In one of the greatest comebacks in political history, Deng began to gain traction with his insistence on economic reforms and liberalizations to guide China toward modernization, and for that matter to more stability. Deng had been rehabilitated by Mao in 1974, a year before the end of the Cultural Revolution. Mao's reason was simple: He had either killed off or otherwise rendered useless any of the old cadres who knew anything about industrialization. Deng was brought back to try to bring some sense back to industrial production. But, as soon as he came back to the halls of power, he began espousing reforms and liberalizations as a means of putting China on the right modernization path. Interestingly, it was during the next few years that Deng's overall strategies for national development would crystallize, even against the backdrop of a Party that really was not ready for such drastic change. Deng persisted, and when giving speeches on the subject around the country between 1975 and 1978, he often cited two things as the keys to China's economic future: First, China had to adopt Western and Japanese technology and scientific practices to achieve industrial modernization. That would make him the first leader in Chinese history to make this point, leaving behind the millennia old belief that China needed to be self-sufficient, independent of, and even aloof from the world's evolving economic systems. His second point changed the world: He continually argued that reforms and liberalizations on the economic side would create the stability China would need to achieve successful overall national development. He was echoing old tenants found in Dr. Sun Yat-sen's Three Principles, as well as those immortalized on Taiwan by President Chiang Ching-kuo. This was a startling turnaround for any Communist leader, and the world began to take note.

But Deng was clearly not without opponents in the CCP. His rise to the top was burdened by those either still wedded to Maosim or conservatives who at least felt the need to block any attempt to take the country down a free market path. The leader of this opposing clique was Li Peng. Had Li emerged as the top leader in 1978-79, and not Deng, the world, not just China, would be a very different place today. Li would not have reformed or liberalized the nation's economic systems. Chances are that China would still be dirt poor en toto, and that all the remarkable progress that has occurred since 1982 would never have happened had the conservatives won that all-important power struggle within the CCP. All Chinese need to be thankful that Deng prevailed.

I do, however, take exception to Deng's belief that adoption of Western science and technology would be (or was) the key to China's modernization. Deng was merely spouting long held Marxist views on how Communism needed the tools of capitalism in its early stages of development, only to turn around and use those tools to defeat capitalism. Having been a career Communist, Deng still had a bit of this rhetorical, if anything else, streak in him. Indeed, it was something much grander than just technology absorption that gave rise to the New China. It was something else Deng did, no matter how unwittingly, that unleashed the Chinese economy. It is one of the most important points made in this book: Deng took the lid off the pot that was holding the Chinese people hostage to Mao's maniacal thought, policies, campaigns and the rest of it. For years that pot had been bubbling over, yearning to bust loose. Finally, it happened with Deng. He took the lid off, and the rest is world history. Deng finally ended the era of ceaseless political movements and became the first Chinese Communist leader to put economics ahead of politics in the grand scheme of national development.

The Chinese people aggressively took that newfound, game-changing strategy and ran with it, going on to create one of the great miracles of human development with the achievement of bringing some three hundred million into the ranks of the middle class and above. That feat is even more admirable when you think that that is the entire population of the USA risen up in a short 30 years! What Deng had unleashed was the power of age-old Chinese entrepreneurialism, never before ALLOWED to flourish in such unbridled fashion. Under Deng, China would go from being the most closed society on earth to one busting out in all directions, and not nearly as controlled as say a fireworks display.

In 1984, on a trip back to my hometown of Tippecanoe in Ohio, I spoke at the local Rotary Club. Viewed as something of a worldly traveler, they always liked to hear my views on current events around the world, particularly in China. It was then that a fellow asked me if the world should continue to fear Chinese communism. I replied by saying no, that what we really needed to fear now was out of control Chinese capitalism! Even then I understood the power that Deng had unleashed. We saw a miniature version of it in Taiwan, and now it was being practiced by a billion Chinese, not a mere 23 million!

When I was in Beijing in 1980, as noted earlier, Deng had only just begun to talk about reforms and liberalizations. Nothing yet had been implemented. China was still the old China, though it was now stabilized following thirty years of constant upheaval at the hands of Mao and the CCP. Several times China was brought to the brink of national collapse, and by this time, well, the people were just plain worn out. A sort of new hope had begun to emerge, but in 1980, it is accurate to say that most people simply did not trust the CCP and the Government. The society was still in something of a holding pattern, probably best described as hopeful that Deng's reforms would occur, but still deeply distrustful of the Party and Government.

Deng's market reforms began with experiments in which export processing zones were created in a tiny village known as Shenzhen, only about an hour into China from Hong Kong, in Guangdong Province. Deng chose

Shenzhen due to its proximity to Hong Kong, where much of the initial wave of investment would originate, and also for its remoteness from the rest of the country. He was committed to reforms, but had to work cautiously within the bounds of the CCP, which still had many pockets of deeply skeptical cadres. Deng was also up against a Communist bureaucracy that had grown used to totalitarian style controls, so he would find it very difficult to move the dial on reform.

Shenzhen became an instant success. It grew faster than any spot in history. The economic prowess of the Mainland Chinese and the experience of Hong Kong quickly proved a great formula for wild success of the free enterprise, free market experiments launched by Deng. In just a few years, Shenzhen had become a major "factory for the word," quickly eating into the exports of Taiwan and Korea. It also quickly grew to be a major metropolitan area in terms of population.

By the mid-1980s, the experiment had spread to other parts of China, almost organically, without Government control. Xiamen rose up, as did much of Guangzhou, which got an early start on liberalizations.

Soon, the likes of Shanghai would want in on the game. The CCP, even Deng, had decided early on to move cautiously with Shanghai, fearing that the city would all too quickly revert back to its old "decadent" self. Not to mention that the city would likely be hard to control once unleashed. Their original suspicions turned out to be perfectly grounded. Once unleashed, Shanghai took off and created a development miracle of its own.

None of this progress was achieved without difficult political challenges standing in the way. Deng constantly had to face the criticism at home and abroad that if his economic reforms were so good for China, then why not go the next step and introduce like political reforms? But Deng always had the right answer to that. Time and time again he repeated his strongly held belief that the economic miracle unfolding could not occur unless China remained stable, and that introducing democracy or other political liberalizations too early would undermine the quest to achieve progress with stability and stability with progress, just as Taiwan, Korea and Singapore had done before China. Deng stuck to his guns on this, despite foreign pressure and pockets of resistance at home.

His view on this can be understood against the backdrop of the student demonstrations in Beijing in the Eighties, culminating with the Tienanmen Incident of 1989. By then, Deng had already relinquished power to a new generation of like minded leaders (Zhao Ziyang and Hu Yaobang). When the students took control of the Tienanmen National Park area in May, the Government initially took what seemed to be an impotent position on the matter—not willing to crack down, but increasingly worried that it was getting out of control and could spread across the country, leading to the dreaded chaos and instability that Deng had been warning against for years. Eventually, after about a month of student occupation of the square, the Government opted for a violent crackdown that shocked the world. Tanks and full military moved in and routed the students out of the square. At the time, reports said more than a hundred were killed, but those numbers have since been lowered to tens. Foreigners, including the U.S. Government, were mortified that their ally Deng would allow such a violent crackdown to occur.

Indeed, Deng's behind the scenes stance on it, and the actions taken by his successors, turned out to be completely aligned with Deng's backbone insistence of maintaining stability so that the Government and Party could deliver on their side of the Social Compact which put economics ahead of politics.

My view on Tienanmen is a bit different than that of most Western observers. For starters, name a foreign country, especially a Western one, who would allow students to turn a national park site into a cesspool? Just how long would hundreds of students, not to mention thousands, be allowed to occupy the Lincoln Memorial? A simple question here: Is such activity legal, or even thought of as tolerable, in Washington, D.C.? Or Seattle for that matter? The answer is absolutely not. Our police would have routed the students much earlier, or perhaps not even have allowed it to happen at all in the first place. Yet China is to be condemned for it? If anything, the Chinese Government should never have allowed the occupy protests to last more than a day. By letting it drag on and grow, it just made the outcome worse.

It all goes back to the idea of the need for stability versus the desire for democracy. Deng and his CCP successor were sticking with what works—keep a tight control on dissent from a tiny minority in society while seeking to deliver on the promise to raise up all of society in economic terms. It is a good bet that the majority of Chinese sitting at home watching Tienanmen unfold on their TV sets were thinking the same thing Americans felt about the hippy movement in the Sixties. Why are these people rocking the boat? Things are good for the first time in 150 years in China. Go away!

Worse yet, the USA displayed its usual penchant for trying to force the democracy drug down the throats of others in the aftermath of Tienanmen. Congress entertained bills that sought to sanction China, its Most Favored Nation trade status was threatened, and so on. The U.S. media wanted heads to roll in China. All I can say is, "there we go again!" The U.S. could have condemned the military force used to end the occupation, but it would have been far more in our national interest to also voice public support, overall, for Deng. We risked undermining his position in China, and that would create an opening for the likes of Li Peng to take power. Fortunately, President George H.W. Bush skillfully managed the crisis, and Deng and his successors, Zhao and Hu, were able to come out of it still on track with their national development strategies.

Deng's Successors

Despite Tienanmen and his obvious tenacity in sticking to his guns on keeping a lid on civil liberties for the sake of national stability, Deng remained a very popular figure abroad throughout his entire tenure. As he slowly began to retreat from the scene, even before health became an issue for him, he guided a group of successors into power who had like-minded notions about the prominence of economics in national development.

His two chosen ones, Zhao Ziyang and Hu Yaobang, proved to be equally astute at stewarding China's continued fast progress in economic development. Tienanmen proved to be a bit testy for them as well, and Zhao eventually was made the scapegoat, and fell from power. But that happened only after he and Hu together had changed the face of Chinese leaders once again. Both wore Western style business suits on a daily basis, and both were totally committed to furthering Deng's reforms. On the face of it, this made them quite popular throughout the world. The diminutive Deng had achieved a sort of pop culture kind of popularity with his easy going style and free-wheeling use of humorous clichés and other forms of open speech. Zhao and Hu took it a step further by showing a more business looking countenance to the world, departing from the political imagery often represented by the formerly omnipresent "Mao" jacket worn by Chinese officialdom.

Later in 1989, Hu would suddenly die of a heart attack, and with Zhao in internal exile over his loose handling of Tienanmen (some in the Party felt he favored the students too much), China was ripe for another leadership change. This time two leaders would emerge who would not only continue Deng's economic reforms, but actually worked to greatly increase the speed and breadth of the reforms. They would be the first leaders in China's modern history to bring backgrounds in economics to the table. These were

Jiang Zemin and Zhu Rongji. Jiang was wedded to further openings to the world, while Zhu managed the economy from his perspective of having emerged out of the Party's highly capitalist clique in Shanghai. Zhu proved to be a highly adept steward of China's rapid march to prosperity and modernization, in so much as anyone could control all of what was going on in the country at the time. Indeed, the out of control capitalism phase that I spoke of earlier was in full-swing by 1990-91.

To its credit, the CCP did institutionalize one important new feature of their soft authoritarian rule—term limits for the top two leaders, namely the President of the country, who also usually holds the title of Chairman of the CCP, and the Premier, who is usually seen less as a figurehead of state and more of a manager of the day-to-day affairs of state. Terms were set at ten years, which might seem long in the eyes of Westerners, but in reality is not a bad length given that China was now completely on the same path of development that Taiwan, Korea and Singapore had used. Meaning, of course, the right path. As China was now in the hands of a string of Dengist leaders, a term of 20 years could also have made sense, if one is following the successful models of those three tigers. In any case, the CCP knew that it could never afford to have another personality cult develop, leading to an all-powerful, megalomaniac leader, like what happened under Mao. Those days were bygone, and the Chinese people welcomed this major political reform. In recent years, I have found that while most Chinese tend to agree with the term limits, and are still supporting one-party rule, they probably also wish the leadership transfers of power could be more transparent. All the secrecy behind the internal votes in the Central Standing Committee rubs a lot of folks the wrong way. But not to the point where they feel a need to outwardly oppose the system (yet).

During the Jiang and Zhu years, China kept on an even keel of fast development while it also avoided any serious problems in the conduct of its foreign affairs. Open to the world and open to furthering the new economic realities in China, neither Jiang nor Zhu would do anything to liberalize the Party's tight grip on the politics and governance of the nation. They kept their eye on the ball of bringing more prosperity to more people as soon as they possibly could. Under their guidance, China maintained growth rates of 8 percent or more for ten straight years, putting the Mainland smack dab in the economic sweet spot that the four tigers used to not only maintain and justify soft-authoritarian rule (that level of growth is proven to keep the folks satisfied with the overall status and direction of the nation) but also used to propel themselves out of poverty and into the ranks of developed economies. Oh, and we never forget here: They also later became robust democracies!

After Jiang and Zhu stepped down due to the new term limits rule, they were succeeded by yet another pair of Party leaders dedicated to the status quo. These were Chairman of the CCP and President of the nation Hu Jintao, and the Premier, Wen Jiabao.

When the two were jockeying for the leadership positions in 2002-03, there was much talk that in tandem they might be a good force for routing corruption and liberalizing the Party, making it more open and accountable to the people. Those turned out be false hopes, although Wen was credited at times for bringing some transparency to the Government. Two examples of this standout: First, he was always pushing to have Government budgets more transparent. And second, on a smaller level though certainly not less indicative of the problem, he was vociferously against the decision to immediately bury the hi-speed railway cars involved in a fatal accident near Wenzhou in 2011. In a move that shocked the world, "someone" in the Party hierarchy ordered the cars to be buried the day following the accident, as if to hide evidence. Wen lost the open battle against that. But the matter increased his popularity, with many Chinese seeing him as a kind, soft-spoken, sort of grandfatherly type leader, who was more open than usual, or at least contrasted with what folks are used to in China.

As their tenure went on, both Hu and Wen would face great challenges at home. Food safety, corruption, housing inflation, foodstuff inflation, unbearable pollution, peasant unrest, ethnic troubles in Xinjiang and Tibet and much more would haunt them on a daily basis. I always joked that only a nut would want to get out of bed every morn to face China's daunting, unprecedented challenges. George W. Bush once remarked that one of his biggest challenges as President was to get up everyday and face the burden of trying to improve the lot of 300 million Americans. Fair enough. But Hu and Wen, and leaders before them and now after them, get up to face five times that many people. Imagine the consequences of suddenly not delivering after

30 years or relative success doing just that?

On the political front, nothing changed at home, and indeed, toward the end of their ten years, many Chinese even felt a little more of a crackdown on the Internet and social media. A few dissidents were arrested for speaking out against the Party, notably Ai Weiwei, an artist in Beijing. This was partly due to the Party's lack of confidence caused by the Arab Spring movement in the Middle East. There, huge crowds of people would gather in large squares on moment's notice thanks to the prevalence of mobile phone devices and the social media that run through them. Chinese leaders saw case after case in which the mob overthrew the Government and leader. Naturally, they recoiled, realizing that in China there are now 700 million cell phone users! (China never really had a public landline system. In the Maoist era, private phones were outlawed. So, when the time came to modernize and move away from that, China wisely decided to skip the costly installation of a nationwide landline system and went straight to cell.).

I tended to be empathetic toward them on this issue. If the chief goal of the society is to remain stable so as to continue delivering economic prosperity to more and more people, then a few draconian measures aimed at either tightening control of the Internet and social media, or at least sending the message that abuses would not be tolerated, is understandable. While I get that, I am also increasingly concerned that support or apathy among young people for such controls is starting to wilt. In this age of hand held communications and now social media, it is increasingly infeasible to maintain control. Just as the fax machine and personal printer helped put the Soviet Union out of business, so will the cell phone also become more than just a thorn in the side of CCP governance. The CCP is right to be worried about it, but on the other hand, the people will likely not be denied these modern conveniences for long. One should hope that China reaches the Stakeholder Society point of development before any Arab Spring type, cell phone-driven movement takes the country asunder.

The point is that Chinese leaders are always forced to walk this tightrope that balances social stability with economic progress. In 2013, this burden passed to two more leaders, President Xi Jinpin and Premier Li Keqiang. Once again, expectations started out high that the two of them would in tandem start tackling corruption and begin liberalizing the Party more. While they have taken certain steps to curtail Government excesses in spending, especially with regard to banquets and gift giving, it now seems apparent that they have fallen into the mode of prior leaders by resembling more caretakers of the status quo than real reformers. More on this subject later.

China Today

When Mao died in 1976, China was still listed as one of the poorest countries in the world. It had a per capita income of only a few hundred dollars per annum. After Deng's reforms in the post-Mao era, a short thirty years in terms of national development in a totally different direction, China now stands with a per capita income of more than $4,000. Some three hundred million people, mostly along the eastern seaboard, have risen to middle class and above, making it the fastest, greatest leap in prosperity ever achieved. Again, the number of lives lifted up out of poverty is equal to or more than the entire population of the United States!

The problem is, some 900 million to a billion people still remain dirt poor, as contrasted with the West, Japan and the four tigers. Taiwan's per capita income, for example, is now at $26,000. Online sources in China list Taiwan as China's most prosperous "province," still ahead of Beijing and Shanghai.

Economically speaking, China is a vastly different place than it was under Mao. Politically, however, the authoritarian nature of the one-party rule in China has not budged. By design. China is unmistakably following in the footsteps of the four tigers, and as long as the CCP continues to deliver on its side of the Social Compact (free economics in exchange for controls on civil liberties and certain rights), then it seems China will likely stay on its current path. The country has already achieved a great deal of personal freedom. Westerners must not be mistaken about this. The average Chinese with the economic means can get out of bed everyday and decide what he or she wants to do with their life. They can move to new opportunities. They can go to school, take vacations, and so on. None of this was true during the Mao era.

This puts China squarely on the path of say a Taiwan,

where basic personal freedoms flourished along side the free enterprise system, in a society that had basically sealed itself off from any potentially harmful inputs from the political side. That is where China is today, and where it should be if it hopes to continue down the path of widening the breadth of prosperity to hundreds of millions more people.

This is not to say there is no dissent or dissidents in China today. There were in the four tigers as well, but the weight of the overall population's support for the Social Compacts in place trumped any noise for political reform coming from a tiny minority of dissidents.

This partially goes back to Dr. Sun's notion that democracy can never easily take root in a Chinese society because Chinese are like grains of sand blowing in the wind. In the West, we say it's like trying to herd cats. Even today nearly every Chinese I speak with on the subject admits that Chinese are currently not suited for democracy, or vice versa, because if they did adopt it, China would immediately break down into chaos with competing interests fighting it out in the halls of parliament to line their pockets and otherwise bring self-interests to the forefront. This is what I call the Latin American trap of democracy, but it also reared its ugly face in Russia as well.

A neighboring country that the Chinese have always taken seriously, Russia proved to be a good example for the Chinese of what not to do. When President Bush One forced Boris Yeltsin to create a democratic parliament before getting any economic aid from the USA, it unleashed powerful, heretofore hidden forces to rise into positions of power afforded by seats in parliament. Russia has stagnated for two reasons: Its parliament is impotent for all practical purposes, and its leader, Putin, is not exactly the right kind of authoritarian leader. He shuts down opponents who have successful businesses, often jailing them and otherwise persecuting them out of the political picture. Chinese see Russia as a mess, as they should. Democracy has done little to pull the average Russian out of poverty. In fact, it stands in the way of the economic reforms and free market policies required for success. Russia is defying the history of what works in national development, and thus it is condemning itself to a bleak future of economic backwardness and instability. What Russia needs desperately is their version of Deng Xiaoping. So far, it ain't Putin.

Chinese also correctly view India as a problem when it comes to setting an example for democracy. India is far poorer than China, and resembles more the Latin American model of a society in which the top two percent control everything and have everything, while the bottom 98 percent continues to languish in the worst imaginable poverty. In addition, a cursory look at India's national and local election history is troublesome. While India likes to call itself a stable democracy, the facts may paint a different picture come election time. The point is that tens of thousands of people have been killed over the years during election seasons in India. You call that stable? The Chinese certainly don't. India is hardly stable, as there is increasing tension between the have nots and the haves, and over religious issues and ethnic issues. The big difference between India and China is cultural, in that Indians tend to be more accepting of their lot (mostly for religious reasons) and tend to be more laid back and less aggressive than the average Chinese in not only seeking a better life, but actually working hard over a lifetime to achieve one. In sum, there is little for China to admire in India, both politically and economically, not to mention culturally.

None of this is to say China is not without its own problems. In fact, many of China's contradictions arise as a result of pressures attributable to its core, historical problem of over-population. I can list ten reasons why China could collapse in the next ten years. Any one of them is enough to cause the collapse, and yet, China must face them all at once!

I am going to run through these quickly, just to demonstrate that China has more reasons than you think for holding fast to its authoritarian nature. Given the stark realities of these major threats to the nation's economy and continued stability, one should only conclude that one-party rule is a necessity now and well into the foreseeable future.

Let's start with China's most basic national threat: Water. You do the math. China has 24 percent of the world's population and less than three percent of the water. Of that three percent, the Chinese Government itself admits that only one third of it is even usable, the rest having been contaminated in one way or another by human, agricultural or industrial pollution. Add to this mix the fact that China's electric grid is mostly fueled by hydro-electric power, and you have another component that zaps the water supply on a huge scale. Water is China's Achilles Heel in the estimation of this observer. And it would not be the first time. In his book WATER, a history, Robert Solomon shows that China's rise as a world power was undermined at least twice in her long history by tremendous shortages of water. It's why the Chinese built the Grand Canal some two thousand years ago, to help bring water from the south to the more arid north. It's why they have plans to build yet another south-north canal. If anything has the power to put sudden breaks on China's growth, it's water. Yet, this problem is not openly talked about, and rightly so in my opinion. Were Beijing to focus on it publicly too much, it would scare the living daylights not only out of the general populace, but stock markets as well.

Next on our list is the general overall lack of resources, especially as this relates to inter-provincial rivalries in China. Foreigners tend to forget that China has been mining and using minerals for nearly five thousand years now, as opposed to say, what? About two hundred years in the continental USA? This naturally means that China is far closer to having depleted its natural resources. It also has had a much larger population over its history consuming these resources. While it can be argued that the Industrial Revolution in the USA and Europe starting in the 1870s caused Westerners to use resources at a much faster rate, it would seem this is still no match for hundreds of millions of Chinese using up resources over millennia.

The problem is two-fold on natural resources. First, provinces are starting to tell Beijing to get lost when it comes to distribution of such things as coal, iron, copper and so on. The provinces are taking a stance against Beijing's vestigial command economy practice of deciding who gets what and who gives what. The northwest areas of Xinjiang and Inner Mongolia are becoming increasingly protective of their natural resources, preferring to have control over them whether for preservation purposes or to have the right to sell them to other provinces as they see fit. This could eventually lead to a state of warfare among provinces for resources. It is one thing that could unravel China's national unity, yet again, as has happened many times throughout her long history.

The second problem with resources is the inflation caused by an increasing lack of resources or the need to import more of them. Either way, market forces are driving up the costs, as are the more costly extraction methods needed to get to the bottom of the resource. The Chinese Government inflation figures are often ignored by the masses, because they feel the inflation at the market everyday, every week, and not as some would hope on a year basis. As with other inflationary pressures, this kind of scourge could serve to keep hundreds of millions more Chinese further away from the opportunity of sharing in the prosperity. Simply put, they are being priced out of the market, perhaps in perpetuity. That presents us with the next big problem in China, the gap between the haves and have-nots.

While such gaps occur in nearly every capitalist society or even mildly socialist country, as with other things related to China, the gap in China is HUGE and growing by the day. My estimate is that some three hundred million people are now living what we would accept as a middle to upper class lifestyle. That leaves just over a billion people close to the poverty line. Unfortunately, the one thing a lot of these poorer masses do have is access to a TV. This means the good life in the cities is there in full view for them to see. The speed with which they can witness and grow to envy the "good life" in China is unprecedented in Chinese history. Couple this with the thought that nearly all of China's past dynastic changes were brought about by agrarian revolutions, and you have the perfect storm forming for another revolution in China. The fact is that it is not at all desirable to be a Chinese leader today. Both Xi Jinping and Li Keqiang get out of bed each day having to face problems that other countries are fortunate to only have to read about. Imagine being a CCP leader today knowing that your former political base, the peasantry, has been left behind in the nation's breakneck race to develop, and that if history is any indication at all of what may come, the CCP is in serious trouble.

This problem is also worsened when resources are considered. It simply is not physically possible for 900 million more Chinese to have cars, air conditioners, refrigerators and so on. It's just not going to happen, and certainly not in the lifetimes of a majority of these people. There simply are not enough resources available. Name the resource, do the math and worry.

I hear reports all the time that a power struggle within the CCP continues to rage over what to do about this dilemma. Since Deng's days, the Party has sold its soul to the capitalist clique, and while it has achieved formidable results in lifting living standards in some parts of the country, it remains very true that most of the country is still waiting in line for its shot at prosperity. And like the farmers before them, today's farmer in China (and even the impoverished suburbanite) feels strongly that the CCP must deliver, or else. China's increasingly more open media are reporting more and more of the violent protests that occur throughout the hinterlands. Farmers crash Party HQs with rakes and hoes, demanding more of the economic pie and other forms of relief in the wake of their having been "left behind." U.S. satellites pick up on many of these protests, further verifying the problem exists and revealing just how widespread it is in China's vast western regions.

For its part, what's the Party to do? If China can maintain its current levels of economic progress, it may indeed get around to helping the rest of the country (one billion people!) rise up. But that seems unlikely for many reasons. The line is too long, the wait too long. At what point might the peasantry snap? Will the poor storm China's urban areas and start taking what they think they should have? This can never be ruled out, which makes it ever more of an imperative for the Party to turn its national development focus west, having pretty much already succeeded in raising up the east.

The problem of haves and have-nots confronting each other violently in the future is not limited to China. Other countries that experience such large gaps in income levels and prosperity levels are also at great risk. These include, but are not limited to, the likes of Brazil, Russia, Indonesia and India. I see mankind coming to blows first over water supplies, then resources in general, with wars over religion and between the haves and have-nots sprinkled in. China is not alone.

Now, not in any sort of order, the next threat to China's march to prosperity is its soon to be bankrupt pension system. One need look no further than Japan and Europe to see the twin effects of an aging population on societies.

The first blow comes when the majority of the population is either retired or nearing retirement age. When that happens, two negative forces kick in. First, consumption drops considerably as those on fixed incomes greatly decrease their discretionary spending. Next, the pension system typically gets turned on its head, with more people taking from it than are putting funds into it. These twin pinchers drastically weigh down the system. In China's case, like everything else related to over-population, the problem is many times worse.

In the next five years, China will have seen its baby boom population reach retirement and take retirement. The problem? You are talking about some 600 million people! As it is currently structured, there is no way on earth that the system is sustainable. Oh wait. There is one way to fix it: young working age people can hand over 90% of their hard earned money in the form of taxes to the government to support the system! Young people in China are starting to figure this out, and it leaves them depressed when thinking about it. This aging population problem has been the main culprit behind Japan's now 20 years of economic stagnation, not to mention Europe's. What will its effects in China be? One can only imagine that the problem would necessarily be magnified many times over. Not even China's pretense of socialism will overcome it.

Worsening the problem is China's draconian one-child policy. While that policy may have been badly needed twenty years ago to stem a still out of control population boom, one of its after-effects, and unforeseen consequences, is now crystallizing. There will be far more retired persons in China than working people. A system designed to have six people supporting the retirement of one person is now in the process of flip-flopping. It is without doubt unsustainable. Again, at some point it is going to put the breaks on China's growth.

Next on the list is debt. While the world likes to focus on debt problems in Europe and the U.S., China has been getting away with a debt problem that may in fact dwarf anything in the West. For starters, because China is not transparent enough about such matters, experts are left guessing much of the time as to the extent of China's overall national and local debt combined. Some say it dwarfs even that in the U.S. Skeptics abound partly due to what occurred in Chongqing, China's largest city, when its Party leader Bo Xilai fell from grace (and power!) two years ago. He was removed for violations of the law and rules on Party behavior, but it was later discovered that he was leaving the city in debt to the tune of some $176 billion dollars. As in U.S. dollars! Few knew about the debt, if that is even possible to fathom. Chongqing had grown stupendously under Bo but now we know he had borrowed just about every penny to achieve that kind of success. China's current leaders are trying to get to the bottom of the debt problem, and have repeatedly asked for a reckoning, a number, on just how high it is. That has not been forthcoming, leaving many financial experts worried about the truth.

A deeper look at the problem is warranted here. Earlier, I argued that China is neither here nor there in terms of being a command economy or a free market economy. The debt issue brings this state of affairs into sharp focus. Why? Because China has developed much of its fantastic, modernistic infrastructure without any regard to market forces. Massive new structures go up all the time, only to be left unused most of the time. The best examples of this are entire cities built on the outskirts of the hinterlands, intended to lure the peasantry into urban work-living environments. These are known as China's ghost cities. They are complete with libraries, sports arenas, countless rows of high-rise condos, parks and much more. The only problem is, not a single person is living in them. I have seen one of these on the outskirts of Baotou in Inner-Mongolia. When you fly in, you see literally countless rows of empty high-rise condos and housing developments. While the Government does have a major policy undertaking of mass urbanization of the hinterlands population, nearly everyone would agree that this approach makes no sense at all. There are no jobs in these cities for tens of millions of immigrants from the hinterlands, for starters.

The second best example of the lack of market forces in infrastructure planning is with sports arenas and stadiums. Every city and town in China seems to have felt the need to have a $400 million arena or stadium built nearby. Most of these are grotesque attempts at Space Age architecture, and if anything is for certain, it is that these structures invariably stick out like sore thumbs. And they are always empty. I am told that most are used once or twice a year. When I relate to my Chinese friends and colleagues that our stadiums and arenas come as the result of hard fought for tax levees on the local population, they are dismayed. In China, multi-million dollar sports facilities fall out of the sky. The point is that massive debt has been accrued by localities and the central government to build all these trappings of modernity and prosperity. And no one, **no one**, knows just how much that debt figure is.

China's lack of transparency is an ongoing issue with financial analysts the world over. Just recently Morgan Stanley reported that it was finding big discrepancies over China's reported export figures, among other things. Morgan Stanley researchers asked China for its export volume broken out by country. Then the team asked the importing countries to list their imported volumes from China. The numbers were way off. Half off! Morgan Stanley, in the same report, said it doubted China's assertions that it would have 7-8 percent growth in 2013. They think the figure is more like half that as well.

The problem is a vestige of the old Soviet style economy. During the Fifties, Sixties and Seventies,

Communist cadres in charge of industrial output would invariably lie about their output figures so as to either give the appearance of meeting unrealistic centrally planned goals, or to show off their prowess in front of Party bosses back in Beijing, in hopes of winning a promotion. Vestiges of this are still around in China's vast network of state-owned companies. It's no wonder that a Western financial firm would sooner or later uncover major discrepancies. So long as the Party bureaucracy remains wedded to the idea of having to look good in front of Party bosses, this problem will persist, and China will continue to have a lack of transparency.

In my own personal observation, coupled with occasional reports on like subjects, I see a China that is way over built. There are massive, completely empty structures all over the place. And some reports indicate that there are as many as 70 million unoccupied condos in China. We know something is wrong when the Central Government continually tries to put the brakes on further development. Other reports consistently warn that China's real estate bubble will greatly dwarf that of say, again, the USA. And there is an awful reason for this. In China, local government and Party officials receive "red envelopes" of cash for allowing development projects to move forward. At least that was the original model for this type of corruption. Now, it's reversed a bit. Here is a common scenario today: A developer puts up Phase one of a massive high-rise housing project. When the first dig occurred, the local officials got their payoffs. This first building is now 20 percent sold out. But what do the officials do? They demand that the developer begin digging Phase Two, so they can keep their flow of payoffs coming. Now, Phase One is say 30 percent sold out, and Phase Two is ten percent sold out (people always want to get in on top floors first, so there are always investors around for these choice units in new developments). But lo and behold, no matter, it's time for Phase Three, solely on the basis of it being bribe time again. Another dig, another red envelope.

To its credit, the Central Government despises such corruption among local officials. It has helped fuel the massive bubble in the real estate market. It's no wonder there are 70 million empty condos around the country!

This makes for a good segue into the next subject; corruption itself. In recent public opinion polls, Chinese have listed food safety as their number one concern. Second is corruption, at all levels of government and the Party.

The "red envelope" culture is as old as the hills in China. In that sense, it has been tolerated as a "normal" feature of everyday life in China for many hundreds of years. China is a culture in which connections matter greatly, and in lieu of connections, you can get things done with under the table cash handouts. It certainly explains why so many low ranking officials in government and the Party can afford to drive BMWs and wear Rolex watches on their US$12,000 salaries!

The problem is hugely widespread, and is known as the "cost of doing business in China" among foreigners. I learned early on that every business plan I prepared for

China required a budget line for "cost of doing business." This is for such things as getting your electricity turned on in a timely fashion, getting your permits at all, and so on. I personally was looking at retail space in a Shanghai department store. The guy in charge of retail space sales told me what the store charged for getting into a spot (like getting on the shelf in the U.S., which is a normal cost). Then he told me to call a friend of his who had recently concluded a deal to find out what the "other" costs might be. I did that, knowing full well that he was referring to the amount of red envelope he would require but not ask for directly. Getting into the space as a normal business was about US$50,000, while the red envelope was advised to be about $10,000. Not from me.

I have many, many other accounts of this over the years. Perhaps the most disturbing are those that involve factories. When building a new one, you can bet that you won't get electric power to it until a pay off has been made.

With regard to corruption of this sort, China is not unlike Africa, where corruption is legion. But China is not near as bad as Africa, where it is reported that oft times 90% of a project's funding gets lost into the pockets of government officials, thereby helping to keep Africa a basket case of development. In China, the corruption nowhere near approaches that level, but I will say that the "cost of doing business" line item in budgets is usually around 10 to 15 percent of the total. And, while this level of corruption may be more of a nuisance than a drag on the economy overall, there is increasing evidence that the Chinese themselves are burning out on it. They are getting tired of the game itself, if not the burden it places on their increasingly tight profit margins. I have heard from more and more Chinese in the past six months that they are getting near a breaking point in allowing the system to persist. Part of it is also their disgust with local officials living the good life off such illegal activity (yes, as culturally institutionalized as they are, bribes are illegal in China).

We're not done yet. China still has more to worry about.

Next on the list is pollution. Not much prompting needed here. China makes the world news all the time with tales of unbelievable pollution of its skies, rivers, underground water supplies, lakes and even oceans. All in all, I have often observed when taking hi-speed trains over long or short distances, looking out the window reveals anything but a beautiful country. To find the China immortalized in paintings and snappy postcards, one need go far into the interior or to remote areas. Otherwise, China is what it advertises itself as: the world's factory. And that China ain't pretty.

Air pollution is becoming the stuff of legends in places like Beijing. More often than not, the capital city disappears in smog so dense that you cannot even see five meters in front of you. Not very healthy, you think? In the first couple months of 2013, the severity of Beijing's air pollution problem reached levels some forty times beyond acceptable levels of danger to humans. Most large cities suffer similar fates at the hands of industrial and automobile pollution. I lived in Jining, in Shandong Province for three years. Jining has a peculiar fate in China. It is near where much of the coal mining is centered for the nation. So, instead of transporting coal to their municipalities around the country, cities in China opt to build power plants near Jining so they can ship the electricity instead of the much more expensive coal itself. Great for them, a horrible calamity for the residents of Jining who endure some of the worst air in the world, almost on a daily basis. Blue skies are rarely seen there, and even though we really liked the people in Jining, we still had to throw in the towel and get out of Dodge. Wuhan and other major industrial cities fare no better much of the time.

Water pollution is of equal concern. With China ruining its water supply from the triple directions of human waste, agricultural overuse and industrial waste, there is a catastrophe in the making. Of the three percent of the world's fresh water supply that China has, two-thirds of that has already been permanently spoiled by pollution. China's breakneck rush to development is often criticized for having left in its trail a country nearly completely trashed. It is true that such development came at a potentially grave cost to the country. But a worse fate was the lid Mao had put on the country. Those lost decades "forced" the Dengist into a position of having to make up time. Plus, taking the lid off suddenly like that necessarily meant that a rush to development would ensue, involving as it were undesirable consequences difficult to control or stop. Hopefully, China will continue to create the national wealth that will be needed to rectify the damage done by pollution in the modernization process, before it's too late. Scientists are already expressing concerns not just about cancer levels rising and the like, but also deformations in babies and such. One of the consequences of the polluted environment is that rich people send their kids to America, Canada or Australia because they do not want them growing up in such an environment in their home country. There are other reasons given for emigration flight, such as the education system's flaws and pressures, but the environment tends to top the list.

As if pollution is not enough to worry the average person, try food safety. As noted earlier, it now tops the list of the public's daily concerns in China. Horror stories abound, and are too many to cover here, but just a couple can bring home the point.

Let's start with the big kahuna, the problem with domestic-made infant formulas, or powdered milks. The Central Government itself reports that some 70% of the formulas tested are either substandard on the whole or even contain dangerous elements (this is also true of bottled water in China). Chinese mothers of newborns are beside themselves. The only way to completely ensure safety is to buy foreign infant formulas, mostly from America or New Zealand. These have to be brought into the country by hand, because the American and NZ brands have production in China, BUT there are a slew of counterfeit producers using those brand names. As a result, mothers do not know whom to trust, other than the surefire purchased abroad-brought into the country by hand fare. Now, however, China is limiting the number of cans or containers that can be brought in. Not sure why, but that is the case.

The second example is as disgusting as it gets. Chinese restaurants have been found (on a large scale) to be using what is known as "di gou you," or gutter oil in their cooking. Are you ready for this? This is oil that is thrown out in the gutter then recollected, literally, down the road for a second go around. Chinese have a famous dish called "hui guo rou," or "return to the pot meat." I think the gutter oil should probably not return to the pot. What say you?

As we have noted all along here, China's worst problems all tend to stem from the population time bomb. The last one to discuss here is agricultural production, and the unthinkable challenges that China faces with regard to it.

Again, it's largely a matter of math. The reason China has resisted mechanizing in the countryside is to preserve employment of hundreds of millions of persons. Obviously, a noble goal. The problem is that the population is aging as a result of a candle burning at both ends (as is quite often the case with any problem in China). On the one hand, young people have been fleeing the countryside for the Promised Land of the big cities, overflowing with jobs (not any more!) and the good life. This leaves mom and dad back on the farm doing all the work. When I travel around on the trains, I make it a point to look out the window for most of the ride. Invariably what you see in the countryside are farms being worked by persons over the age of 60, many seemingly in their seventies if not eighties. This lopsided farm population will not last long. At some point, it may be necessary for mechanization to supplant labor. But what if the planning for that crossover is off, by say a few years? A major catastrophe could result, not unlike the Great Leap Forward, though certainly not as heinous or ill thought out. The CCP is very busy keeping its eye on this problem, as it should. The breaking point is coming, it's just a matter of whether the Government's timing is on or not. Adding to the pressure to mechanize at exactly the right moment in time is the Government's policy of encouraging peasants to move to urban areas. In the past five years alone an astounding five hundred million people have migrated to cities, making it history's greatest human migration of all time. Again, who wants to get out of bed every morning to face such challenges? It's time for the world to be more empathetic to China, its leaders, its Government and yes, the CCP, too.

Interestingly, however, not all of China's critical ills evolve from the population time bomb. Some are related to culture. One of these that deserves mention is the fact that China is also neither here nor there in terms of being a rule of law society. This is a problem that could eventually undermine everything, and as such, needs to be discussed here.

China's long cultural heritage is strong, so strong in fact, that in some cases it is nearly impossible to bend or change. Over the millennia, China has relied on personal connections, imperial fiat and other non-legal forms of coercion to keep the people in line. In this model, the Government largely looks the other way at many behaviors that we in the West would consider unlawful. Bribery/corruption is one of them, but the lack of the rule of law as a whole is the one that threatens stability in China. While Western nations pride themselves on the rule of law, Chinese tend to see it as an inconvenience that, if it does not suit their individual whims, just goes ignored.

This problem manifests itself in broad daylight on any street in any city in China . Its worse, of course, in the hinterlands. Examples of this are such things as unruly traffic, civil disrespect for others, and other petty forms of lawlessness. Most foreigners shake their heads and move on. Others want to shout at the Chinese. But none of that is useful in a culture that has been going about this way for hundreds if not thousands of years.

Unruly traffic is one thing, but it is nothing compared to what happens when the lack of the rule of law seeps into business activity. Taiwan and Hong Kong came before them sure enough, but the scale of Mainland activities such as counterfeiting products is, like anything else good or bad in China, off the charts. Counterfeiting or piracy of products happens to be a "natural step" on a nation's economic development. First you take on OEM, producing for others, then gradually you learn to produce the same products yourself. Those who are able move to their own branded products, while the majority opt to become pirates. The Chinese Government continually asserts that it is cracking down on counterfeits, but that is starkly untrue, and there is an in-your-face example to prove it. In

Beijing, foreigners flock to a building complex called the Silk Road Market. There, you can buy any brand of anything in the world for far less than the retail price that brand commands in the real world. If Beijing were serious about cracking down on counterfeits, wouldn't it just simply shut down the building? It's right there in broad daylight.

The problem is (most likely) that a red envelope again trumps the rule of law and to Chinese, there isn't much wrong with that picture. They, too, are big consumers of such goods.

The lack of the rule of law sounds like it should be a contradiction in a society that is authoritarian. Authoritarian by its very nature suggests *too much* control, rather than *too little* control. This is, to be sure, one of China's great contradictions today. The CCP no doubt has the power to arrest a dissident or make someone disappear, but it does not have the authority, or inclination, to enforce traffic laws?

Foreigners mistakenly view the CCP as all powerful in China, a Big Brother that controls everything. If that were so, why is so much of China out of control?! Foreigners who live outside Beijing see very little Communist control or even influence in the daily life of the citizenry. In Shanghai, one would swear that there is no Communist Party around, at least in the usual sense that it conjures up. Is the CCP merely selective in what it enforces? Or have things really gone back to culture mode, meaning, the grains of sand are blowing in the wind again after being let loose from the silos they were in during Mao?

During the Mao era, the lack of the rule of law didn't matter so much as the whole society was under the iron fist of the Party and it sought to control every aspect of the people's lives in textbook totalitarian fashion. There was no justice system to speak of, and certainly the law was whatever the Party said it was.

That Party, and that system, are long gone in China, thank goodness. And, while anomalies still occur throughout the system on a daily basis, there is no question that China has worked feverishly to move the dial toward the rule of law. Less and less is the society relying on personal relationships to conduct matters normally associated with the law. Less and less is the influence of the red envelope culture, though it still has a long way to go. And, with regard to such things as social civility and traffic law, well, my experience in Taiwan shows that these are problems that are gradually overcome. As the majority becomes more affluent, it starts to take on a more civil nature. This is a natural evolutionary process that, like everything else in China, will take much longer due to the population.

I have rather quickly run through this list and discussion of a series of challenges that threaten China's future. Note that not a one of them involves a challenge from beyond China's own borders. Which leads to a VERY important point made by Hu Jintao. Hu told an audience of foreigners some years back that China's biggest contribution to the world, and mankind, would be the successful management of its own population. Bingo. That sums up in a nutshell why China does not threaten anyone else. Its domestic challenges overwhelm it on a daily basis. Hu is telling an important truth about China.

My point in running through this list parallels Hu's. With all of these potentially apocalyptic threats bearing down on it, China has no choice but to remain a soft authoritarian system that maintains stability by continuing to deliver the good life to as many people as possible and as quickly as possible. The lack of resources needed to achieve that noble goal may eventually undermine the whole process, leading to who knows what kind of social breakdown between the haves and have-nots, and between the provinces.

There probably is not a soul in China who would prefer going back to the chaos and totalitarian gulag of the Maoist era. I have met very few individuals who desire the return of *that* Communist Party. With all of its warts today, the CCP is a far cry better than it was during Mao's reign of terror and lost decades. Indeed, you occasionally come across a laborer over the age of 60 who will tell you that he yearns for the Party of old, the one that stood up for the small guy, poor guy. There are such people who scold the CCP for having sold out to the Capitalists in the name of enriching their own pockets. Still, when further queried, these types go on to say that they are talking about the original ideals of the CCP, not the nutcase Mao. Fair enough. Overall, however, even most of the disenfranchised peasantry is better off since Deng's reforms took root as well, since the communes were shut down and they switched to tracks of land that farmers are given to till to their own designs and money making schemes.

Which leads us to one of the most glaring, and by far most sensitive contradictions of the post-Mao era in China. The fact that the CCP has achieved great success since Mao thanks largely to having thrown its own founding Marxist-Leninist principles right out the back door and onto the ash heap of history (as Reagan once called the fate of Communism). Imagine that. A Party throwing out everything it stands for, goes on to achieve great developmental success, and yet still pays lip service to the very principles it threw away?

Has this ever happened before in history? Imagine what would ensue if the Republican Party in the USA threw out its commitment to democracy, freedom and so on, so as to maintain its power or to achieve power? Or the Democrats doing the same with theirs? Ridiculous, totally.

But that is exactly what has happened in China. The Communist Party still leads the country. It has all the political power. It pulls many of the levers of socio-economic development in the country. Yet there is no communism in China. None. Nada. Nichevo. And nearly everyday, in its official media somewhere, somehow, the CCP still pays lip service to Mao, Marx and Lenin. Why the subterfuge? What gives?

Its simple. Their "out" is that they now refer to Communism as a goal of the distant future. That makes it irrelevant to people today, so they rightly ignore it. In addition, the CCP has a new name for what it does stand for: Socialism with Chinese characteristics. This is constantly repeated to ensure that a tie back to Communism will always be top-of-mind for the masses. That is because in the Marxist playbook, socialism is the phase that leads to the ultimate goal of Communism.

In my view, however, the word games are going to haunt the CCP in the future. More and more Chinese will not like the idea of having a Communist Party around. For one, it hurts China's image in the world. I often find myself explaining this to Chinese I meet around banquet and lunch tables, or on hi-speed trains. When a Chinese complains about how China is viewed negatively all the time in the rest of the developed world, I remind him or her that the Chinese Government itself says everyday that it is Communist. Communism is a bad word in the West, and since most people don't understand or know much about China, they naturally assume the worst about a so-called Communist society. It is humiliating to most Chinese I know that their nation is lumped together with the other bad boys on the planet, namely Iran, North Korea, Russia, Cuba and maybe even Venezuela these days. The Chinese are tired of having so much trouble getting visas around the world. That is purely the fault of the CCP for insisting on calling China Communist or relating anything having anything to do at all with Communism to China. It's a major case of shooting yourself in the foot, like, everyday.

I have often suggested that the solution to this image problem is quite simple, yet probably impossible to bring about. All that needs to be done is for the CCP to change its name. Get rid of the Communist rhetoric once and for all. Call a spade a spade. China is not Communist, so stop saying it is or wants to be.

I take this argument a step further by also insisting that China needs to change its national flag. Why? Because the current one represents the Communist era in China. It is a Soviet import, like the ideology itself. Why would the great nation of China use a symbol of an imported ideology as its national flag? That is terribly unfortunate. China has a millennia old existence. Its flag should attempt to identify with that entire picture, rather than just a snapshot of a 30-year period, that, to make matters worse, is perhaps the period Chinese would like most to forget. Yes, the flag has to go. In the London Olympics, I observed that the Chinese uniforms were adorned with dragons instead of the yellow stars of Soviet days past. Could this have been intentional? Is there someone on the inside also clamoring for a new national symbol on a new flag, one that represents as best one can the entirety of China's ancient yet still thriving civilization? I certainly think so, and hope so. In any case, China today should not have any vestige of the former Soviet Union as its national symbol. Again, as a son-in-law of China, I am embarrassed by this, and hope that more and more Chinese will see it the same way, for what it is.

The same goes for the Hammer and Sickle symbol that, while not as predominant as it used to be, sticks out more and more like a sore thumb when it is occasionally seen in China. Again, contradictions. Why have a Hammer & Sickle symbol next to Nike, Sony and Coca-

Cola? Far from being a symbol of pride for anything in China, that symbol is not only incongruous with the realities in China today but it is also a reminder of a terrible past. Who needs that in China?

But the main thing China absolutely needs to do so as to win international respect, is to take Mao Zedong off his pedestal in China. This is a problem that drives me batty beyond belief. One and a half billion Chinese people have absolutely lost their minds if they do not understand this issue.

If we simply go by the numbers alone, Mao is up there with Stalin and Hitler as the most brutal mass killers of all time. In fact, Mao crimes against humanity dwarf those two. In Mao's case, it wasn't simply killing off those opposed to his reign, but was more so the case of tens of millions of people dying as a result of his maniacal economic policies.

What nation, what people on earth, would continue to respect and worship in any way, form or fashion such a leader? Unfortunately, most Chinese do.

It can be argued that they have been brainwashed over the years into believing in a Mao that never existed in real life. That is partially true. The brainwashing does go on in schools and in the state-run media. But via the tradition of story telling and now newfound pockets of academic freedoms, Mao's sins have been increasingly aired in China. Yet, still, many are willing to give him a pass, insisting that his contributions to modern China outweigh his crimes against the Chinese people, the Chinese nation, and China's culture.

How could this be? What leader in the West could survive the deaths of ten people let alone a hundred million? It is completely inconceivable to the Western mind that a failed, murderous leader of this proportion could survive the test of time and remain on pedestals, literally, throughout the country. I would not argue for a rewrite of history or the erasure of Mao from history books. No, not ever. The point is the pedestal. Why do Chinese worship the single deadliest leader in the history of mankind? How do they ever expect to win international approval for that?

This is the single greatest embarrassment for the Chinese people today.

But here is where I go off on a tangent that most Westerners don't consider. While Mao needs to be toppled once and for all, I would not agree that the same is true for the CCP. And, while no one wants the Party of the 50s, 60s and 70s to return, it is a fact that a massive majority of Chinese have bought into the leadership role of today's CCP, SO LONG as it continues to deliver on economics. I buy into this. Also, this is not to say that the average Chinese doesn't see much room for improvement in the CCP. To the contrary, such issues as corruption and greed need to be addressed, and soon.

10 CONCLUSION: AN ATTEMPT AT SUMMATION BY DAVE ~~JR.~~ 2.0

Over the years my father-in-law spoke often about his desire to write the book you now hold in your hands. Unfortunately, he was unable to complete the work and it wasn't until after his passing on August 28, 2016 that I ever got the opportunity to read it. There was no question in the minds of the family that we should see it published, but we suspected that the giant blank white space following the heading "Conclusions" might be something of an obstacle. As one of the very first people to read his book I suppose I've claimed the honor of scribbling in his white space. Dave often referred to me as "Dave Jr."; even before I married his daughter. I typically countered with a correction; "Dave 2.0". The implication of an upgrade or improvement is obvious (and intentional), but as many of us know and Apple products have so often demonstrated, a newer version isn't always the same as an improvement. So, I'm going to do my best to dot some I's and cross some T's, but don't be too surprised if you find that the headphone port is missing.

Fortunately, I have been given license by the only opinion that matters, the author's daughter, to keep this brief. So, strap in for your favorite chapter…the short one.

The title of this book can be shocking. It seems to go against everything that those of us in Western society have believed all our lives. At first glance it seems to suggest that democracy is a bad thing. If you read "Just Say No to Democracy" and found it shocking I hope you also found it curious. Hopefully, you read enough of the book to pick up on the unprinted "…for now" that could have followed. The argument Dave makes is not that Democracy is bad or that it should not be a goal for developing countries. The argument is that Democracy should not come first or at the expense of economic prosperity.

Dave believed that economic progress should be the highest priority of any developing nation. In order for a true and lasting Democracy to be possible there must first be a solid economic foundation. The argument put forward in this work is that Democracy may not be the best path toward economic prosperity. The exchange of power from one party to another can make it difficult to affect lasting change in the early stages of nation building. The "Colombia is Passion" campaign is an excellent example of this idea. You have two parties which want to see a prosperous Colombia, but two different ideas on how to achieve success. There are too many cooks in the kitchen. One good idea (or good leader) could carry a nation out of poverty and into prosperity, but competition for power and self interest undermine the stability necessary for continued growth. Over the period of 2004 to 2012, the "Colombia is Passion" campaign saw an increase in GDP from about 117 billion USD to about 370 billion USD. In the time since, GDP has fallen to around 283 Billion USD (2016). What might have happened if someone hadn't tried to fix what wasn't broken?

As promised, I give you the shortest chapter yet. I probably haven't adequately summed up Dave's thoughts, but for those of you wanting more I would encourage you to read the more expansive summary beginning on page 1.

Thanks for reading.

ABOUT THE AUTHOR

Although Dave Lightle was born and raised in Tipp City Ohio, this small but beloved city could not contain him and his dreams took him around the world. After graduating Tippecanoe High School, where he remains a legend to this day, he attended Dartmouth College in Hanover, New Hampshire where he earned a Bachelor of Arts degree in Sino-Soviet Area Studies. He spent half of his college years abroad, and was among the first group of American college students to study in both the Soviet Union and People's Republic of China. He spent six months attending Leningrad State University and received a certificate for Russian Language and Culture; nine months attending National Taiwan Normal University and three months attending Peking University where he received certificates for Chinese Language and Culture.

During his professional career, he continued to globetrot and brought a well-rounded perspective on national economic development to his branding and promotional work. Dave became the leading authority on country branding and promotion and was at the forefront of this unique niche in international marketing and branding for nearly 35 years. He earned his stripes in economic development while working for the Taiwan Government Information Office as the International Affairs Adviser and promotion agencies such as China External Trade Development Council (CETRA) as an independent consultant for more than 15 years combined, and is widely recognized as the architect of the Made in Taiwan image crafted during the late Eighties and into the Nineties. Subsequently, he was brought in as an adviser and consultant for Thailand's government during the 1997 Asian Financial Crisis, Colombia's nation branding (Colombia is Passion!) which helped open its doors wider to foreign tourism, foreign investment and exports, and similar projects for Panama.

He spent the last decade of his life aggressively promoting Dayton Ohio as the Home of the Wright Brothers. He and his partners established The Wright Brothers USA, LLC and had been appointed by the Wright Family Foundation as the exclusive, global licensor for The Wright Brothers trademark. A sliver of that effort included creating a line of Wright Brothers products to include flight jackets, aviator sunglasses and watches, travel bags, and also city bikes, which are central to the Wright Brothers' Wings to Wheels story (http://thewrightbrothersusa.com/). Today this work continues to be carried out tirelessly by his partners.

Dave passed away unexpectedly while on a business trip in China on August 28, 2016. He is survived by Chenya, his wife of 37 years, daughters Kristy and Keri, and five grandchildren.

9 781722 458744